Art
JOURNALS
&
Creative Healing

Restoring the Spirit through Self-Expression

BEVERLY MASSACHUSETTS

QUARRY BOOKS

Sharon Soneff

with Journaling Worksheets by Mindy Caliguire

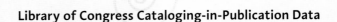

First published in the United States of America by Quarry Books, a member of Quayside Publishing Group
100 Cummings Center
Suite 406-L
Beverly, Massachusetts 01915-6101
Telephone: (978) 282-9590
Fax: (978) 283-2742
www.quarrybooks.com

ISBN-13: 978-1-59253-364-0
ISBN-10: 1-59253-364-7

10 9 8 7 6 5 4 3 2 1

Cover and Interior Design:
Laura H. Couallier,
Laura Herrmann Design
Photography:
Glenn Scott Photograpy

Printed in Singapore

Library of Congress Cataloging-in-Publication Data

Soneff, Sharon.
 Art journals and creative healing : finding restoration through self expression / Sharon Soneff.
    p. cm.
 ISBN 1-59253-364-7
 1. Diaries--Therapeutic use. 2. Art therapy. I. Title.
 RC489.D5S66 2008
 616.89'1656--dc22

                    2007025226
                    CIP

"Change is life giving. It helps us grow into someone greater than we already are."
–Author unknown

[ad·ven´·ture]

Hope

In loving memory of fellow artist and contributor, Mary Zakrajsek, whose inspiring faith and impassioned art accompanied her through many valleys and then to her heavenly home.

Contents

Introduction

JOURNALS SERVE MANY WORTHY PURPOSES—to document major events, capture fleeting moments, develop raw ideas, even to chronicle what you dreamed last night. But has it ever occurred to you that a journal could be used to assist with, and promote, health and healing?

Medical research has long supported the premise that journal-keeping has curative benefits and can improve our overall well-being. Emotional hurts, physical suffering, and even constructive growth can all be approached and understood through the routine use of a journal. But what about the kindred practice of using art to facilitate healing? Might the use of color, form, and gesture provide another piece of the health and healing puzzle? Indeed, art therapy is used in many clinical settings as a treatment for numerous serious maladies, both emotional and physical. Art has been shown to unlock areas of the subconscious, offering a way to excavate and release even deeply buried hurts. Just as beneficial is the use of art as a coping mechanism for life-threatening illness, chronic pain, or even just the common, nagging worries of life. *Art Journals & Creative Healing* explores the combination of these two therapeutic exercises—the written expression with the artistic one—resulting in a venue for pushing beyond difficult human experiences to a place of newfound wisdom, peace, comfort, joy, health, and healing.

Although the assertion that an artful journal can advance health and healing might not be entirely mystifying, knowing where to begin with such a healing journal might be a complete mystery! How do we employ this unique medicine for the mind, soul, and body, outside the clinical setting? In the pages between these covers, a generous offering of journals, combining candid personal journaling and varied creative expression, provides the inspiration and guidance to make your own healing journal. *Art Journals & Creative Healing's* personal accounts of struggle and triumph, and the fanciful journals that served as companions along the way, will inspire you to try your own healing journal, entirely unique to *you, your life,* and *your form of expression.*

There is a wisdom in this beyond the rules of physic.
A man's own observation, what he finds good of and
what he finds hurt of, is the best physic to preserve health.

—SIR FRANCIS BACON

My Story

My story of healing is just like my life: a work in progress. What I am confident of, now, is that you can never be confident of what life will bring your way. Like a string of daily surprises, life gives us a glistening bead of unexpected joy one moment and an unusual stone of difficulty the next. But strung together, they represent a rich, disparate, multifaceted, and beautiful life, one that adorns each of us with the spectacular uniqueness and richness of the life we've lived.

I did not aspire to become the mother of a child with Asperger's syndrome, and yet parenting my remarkable son has offered me more delight and pride than I otherwise could have known. I did not seek to walk alongside my husband through painful years of staving off alcoholism and chemical dependence. And yet the courage, restraint, and strength I have witnessed in him have resulted in a profound love, immense admiration, and deep respect that might not have been earned in any other way. I did not desire to see my beloved father die a slow, debilitating death from a series of crippling strokes and devastating brain hemorrhages. Yet watching death steal not one fraction of Dad's honor or legacy made me learn how weak death really is. I have imperfect, strained, and even severed relationships. I have sequestered heartaches and sadness. I have had my share of ugly inner wars—battles with perfectionism, self-concept, depression, and anger: traits that were never on my target list. And yes, I have the crazy, chaotic, and unpredictable stresses of everyday life: the deadlines and pressures of my business, mingled with the shopping lists, dirty dishes, piles of laundry, carpool tasks, and school committees familiar to every other working mom.

What have invariably been my companions throughout these sequences of the unexpected, though, have been journals. Sometimes incredibly artful and detailed, other times modestly simple and scrawled, these journals have brought me revelation, calm, solace, and circumspection. A work-in-progress journal is the perfect complement to my work-in-progress life, bringing me continuous, work-in-progress restorative health.

—Sharon Soneff

Health and Healing for the Emotions

Finding Peace in the Midst of Emotional Turmoil

FINDING PEACE IN THE MIDST OF EMOTIONAL TURMOIL may sound a bit like finding the proverbial needle in the haystack. But, truly, it is much more available than that.

Peace, calm, and resolve are often found in the sweet, quiet moments garnered for introspective journaling. Simply structuring an environment that fosters real and honest reflection (a private, undisturbed space and time) helps breed tranquility. Furthermore, that tranquility will be compounded by the rhythmic qualities of simply creating. Brushing paint in back-and-forth strokes, dipping a calligraphic pen in an inkwell, punching out shapes, and peeling off stickers all supply a tactile distraction in which the hands are busy and the mind is free. In this precise place of mental liberation, and out of this realm of inaudible expression, a healing balm is concocted from your own artistic well and applied, not just to paper but to your soul. So little is required for this to occur—instruments of expression

(pens, colored pencils, paints, markers, or charcoal) and a surface onto which they can be applied (a purchased journal, a sketch pad, cardboard sheets, canvas).

But the greater requisite is the attitude you bring with these materials. You must come with the understanding that:

- *This is not the time for making masterpieces.* All creative expression is safe and beautiful in the space of a healing journal, in which imperfection is desirable. Imperfections add character and tend to be more honest in their impulsivity. Quick work is telling work. Dare to be urgent in your execution, so that you can be revealing and compelling in the process.

- *Your journaling need not be coherent or complete;* it need only be honest. These pieces are not created for an audience, Your journal is a haven for partial thoughts, and even single words that resound with you.

- *For this to be effective you must make yourself vulnerable.* Remove all judgment-making when expressing and articulating on paper. Unguard your heart.

There can be no knowledge without emotion. We may be aware of a truth, yet until we have felt its force, it is not ours. To the cognition of the brain must be added the experience of the soul.

—ARNOLD BENNETT

My Story

After repeated, intense seasons of hectic pace, painful setbacks, and life's disappointments, my husband and I came to a difficult discovery—our interior lives had been neglected. Hidden beneath the fog that had become our life, my soul had shriveled up along the way. My life of ministry and caretaking had become a laundry list of duty and obligation. This feeling of emptiness came to a head when, for two entire months, I lay in bed suffering from severe vertigo. I felt empty and useless. During this forced period of rest from responsibilities, I began to recognize the dysfunction I had accepted as my reality. All I knew is that I didn't want to live life that way. I genuinely wanted—needed—things to be different.

Journaling, reading "soul books," connecting in authentic relationships, taking time away—all life-giving practices—became an integral part of my life in which I ultimately found restoration, renewal, and refreshment for my own soul.

—Mindy Caliguire

So Much to Gain

JOURNAL BY **Rachel Denbow**

EVERY CHOICE IN LIFE SEEMS TO BRING WITH IT AN ONSLAUGHT OF POSSIBILITIES and emotions: hopes for "could-be" successes and fears for the "might-be" failures. Weighing the potential outcomes can be paralyzing. Moreover, acting on, and then embracing, the actual consequences can be emotionally overwhelming. An art journal becomes a haven in which you can consider your choices, make your move, and contemplate the end result, be it a payoff or a pitfall!

The decision to make a cross-country move is weighted with both risk and potential. Accompanying the allure of starting anew in a fresh environment are the difficulties of feeling isolated and estranged from your previous operating systems and home comforts. Acknowledging and recording the changes taking place lends tremendous insight to the conflicting emotions arising from this monumental adjustment. The journal also offers a place in which to account the discoveries made in a new state (in this case, a new geographical state and a new state of mind) and helps the writer appreciate the adventures and positive strides along the way.

ABOVE A montage of snippets resting on swaths of acrylic paint chronicles thoughts about an emotionally trying cross-country move. A photo serves to document and set the scene for the new chapter in this artist's life.

BELOW With no inhibitions, emotions spill out in an amalgam of strokes, shapes, and hues. An examination of the safe places of childhood spurs constructive thinking about how a safe place might be carved out and created in adulthood. Supplemented by jotted thoughts and lists, the end result is a journal entry that yields clarity and even points to action.

CREATIVE TIP

Try punctuating your art journals with ordinary office supplies. Paper clips, sticky notes, staples, and label tape can all be employed to accent or attach your journaling.

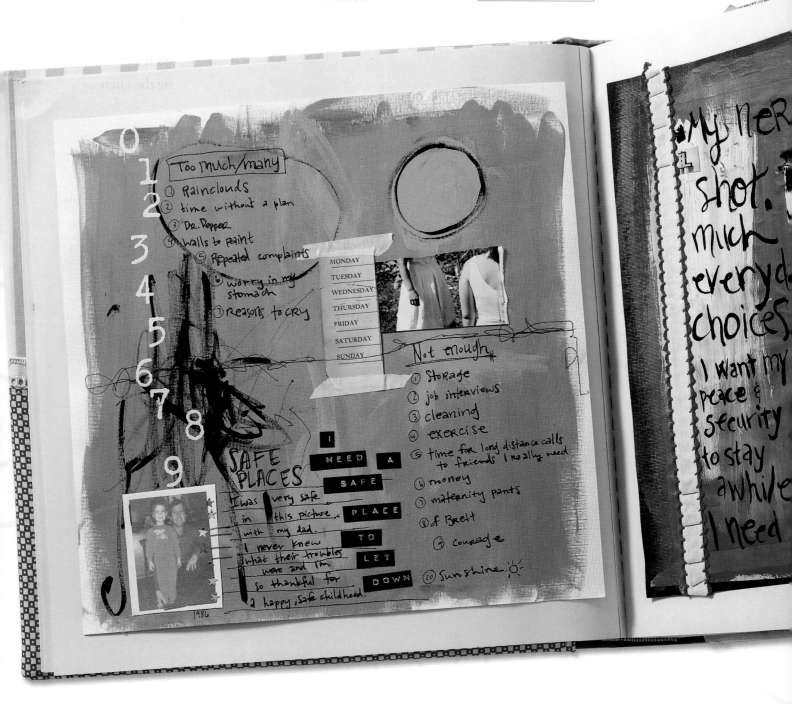

*And the day came when the risk to remain tight in
a bud was more painful than the risk it took to blossom.*
—ANAÏS NIN

My Story

OPPOSITE Rough sketches coupled with doodled words and phrases unite to manifest desire and empowerment to make sense of a new, and even radically different, environment.

Ever since I was in high school, I have wanted to live in an urban environment. So, when my husband started talking about moving from central Oklahoma to Seattle, Washington, for graduate school, I was quickly on board. We talked, prayed, and planned for two years before we were able to make the move. About three months before leaving, we found out we were expecting our son, Sebastian. The realization that we'd be making such a major adjustment without the support of friends and family weighed heavily on me, but I tried to focus on the excitement of a new start.

In Seattle, we faced a number of challenges. The rent for our new apartment was three times more than the rent of the house we had been living in, and we had only the hope that my husband would find a better-paying job within the first two or three months of moving. Our arrival coincided with a record-breaking three weeks of nonstop rain. We had to adjust to the incredible heating bills for our uninsulated apartment, the Laundromat that never dried our clothes, the constant gray skies, and having no friends and a baby on the way. Being at home alone on the computer all day looking for jobs left me feeling sadder than I'd felt in a while. One day, I forced myself to get my journal and art supplies out of our unpacked boxes. I spread everything out on my kitchen floor and opened the blinds on the floor-to-ceiling windows to make it as bright as possible. I watched the traffic on the I-5 across the water and started to put words and colors to my mood.

Sometimes, I feel guarded in my journaling. I think of the access we have to Anne Frank's journal, all these years later, and how she never wrote in it with the intent to share it with the world. Other times, I know that, if I'm not honest in my art, I'm robbing myself of the healing it can bring. So, I decided to start without the expectations of style and composition guiding my work. For the next three weeks, I left my supplies out on my desk, so I wouldn't have an excuse to avoid journaling. I was able to be as raw as I'd been in a long time and not pretend everything was okay. Having an outlet when I didn't have access to close friends and great conversations over coffee helped me make it through the shock of so much change. Things didn't get much easier that year, but we learned to adapt. We eventually made great friends, found some wonderful spots in the city, and welcomed our beautiful son to the prettiest summer weather we'd ever seen.

— Rachel Denbow

Beneath the Surface

JOURNAL BY Jamie Harper

DEPRESSION IS A COMMON PLIGHT, LURKING, often in silent pain, on every street and neighborhood, in every city around the globe. The shame and embarrassment so many equate with this severe despondency often correlates to an unmet standard of perfection, to which we often seem to subscribe. Whether caused by external circumstances or a chemical imbalance, depression is no cause for indignity. Unfortunately, the mechanisms we use to protect ourselves when in this state tend to promote the isolation that only deepens the depression.

Beginning the battle against depression consists largely of admission, perhaps privately at first, in the sheltered confines of a creative journal. By moving out of the shadow of withdrawal and guilt, we can begin to cast off depression and exchange it for the illumination of acknowledgement and then action. Employing words and color are fun and inviting ways to begin this necessary step of identification. With the absence of intimidation (in a journal, there is no one to please or serve or accommodate), journaling stimulates the divulgence of emotions. Feelings we might otherwise tightly withhold pour out without restraint.

LEFT Free-flowing thoughts give way to life-altering epiphanies. A quick glance at the journaling shows the progression of emergent thought: "lost and alone" moves toward "I need help!"

What Lies Beneath the Surface?

LEFT This free—form journal employs an underlying question to induce the observations that follow. An acetate box above the artist's photo encases dirt and creates a metaphor for the excavation necessary to find the answer to the question, "What lies beneath the surface?"

NO NeVeR satisfaction

Distortion

PAIN

travel or passage from one place to another

journey

What lies beneath. Have a happy str... underneath is sad... and a constant within myself. Dont be fooled by my exterior. look be...

BA

ABOVE A peephole in the journal's cover (seen here from the embellished underside) provides a glimpse from the exterior into this soul-searching plunge. A diverse assortment of materials (from printed twill to magazine clippings) communicates the search for a reprieve from pain, dissatisfaction, and sadness.

OPPOSITE Sometimes a simple statement, born out of the journal's creation, can become a mantra for healing. In the spirit of self-analysis, the revelations from journaling can sometimes be cynical, but often the result is a self-formulated affirmation to live by.

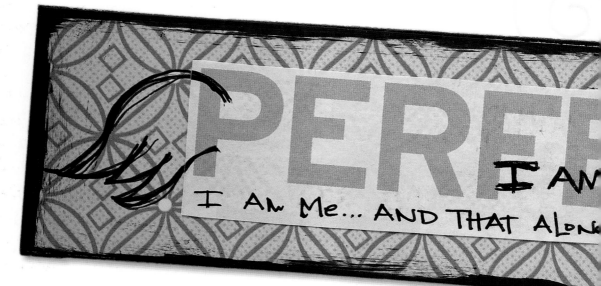

PERFE... I AM

I AM Me... AND THAT ALON...

My Story

For me, depression was not a gradual thing, not something that one might mistake for something else—it was thrust upon me. I was nineteen, and my husband and I had been married only a month when we discovered I was pregnant with my first child. I was elated at the thought of starting our family, but that elation was soon tempered by the onset of physical ailments. From the beginning, I was so sick that I spent almost the entire nine months of pregnancy in bed, and no medications helped. I had been an aerobics instructor, sometimes teaching four classes a day, but eventually I had to give that up. Being at home all day, so sick that it sometimes hurt to breathe, I spiraled downward into a deep depression, a depression that held fast for nine years. Medication helped, but it had many side effects. I had to find something else that would help, but what? Then it came to me . . . art! I missed sketching and drawing, but I often lost interest in art pieces that required a huge time investment to create. It was then that I turned to memory books, art journals, and any small project that I could finish in a short time frame. The art gave me so much more than an outlet. It allowed me to explore and express my feelings, and through the writing came healing and understanding. Yes, I did need medication, but medication alone could not heal me. I needed to be a part of the healing, and reading my own words allowed that healing.

— Jamie Harper

The Naked Truth

JOURNAL BY **Cheryl Manz**

WHEN THERE IS A LARGE GAP BETWEEN PERCEPTION AND REALITY, it causes stress, conflict, and even mental and physical illness. Closing this gap by unclothing the myths and seeing our naked selves is the premise of this journal. Truly, perspective-taking is such a useful skill; under the umbrella of remaining objective and teachable, examining how others might see us allows us to compare our heart state against what we actually convey to others. When the two are juxtaposed, we can bring them better into alignment, narrowing that rift in perception versus reality. We learn not to hide behind false myths that we might purposefully or unintentionally project but rather to act in an honest reflection of our true selves.

Try formatting your own lined journal with enumerated myths. Enhance that perspective-taking experience by finding personal photos that address those myths, and then begin to look at the underpinnings of your communications to others. A healing process will occur as you are able to dispel myths, first on paper, and then in your daily actions.

LEFT A rubber band tightly secures this trendy purchased journal. A few simple adornments—a silk flower, a button, and letter stickers—help to personalize it.

RIGHT By writing an introduction to your journal, you can create a mission statement for what will be accomplished in its pages. A date and signature denotes a covenant and a seriousness of intent to find inner truth.

BELOW Mixing artplay with analysis helps to make sense of difficult realities. This journal's hard, graphic lines are softened by fuzzy felt shapes and curvaceous rub-ons.

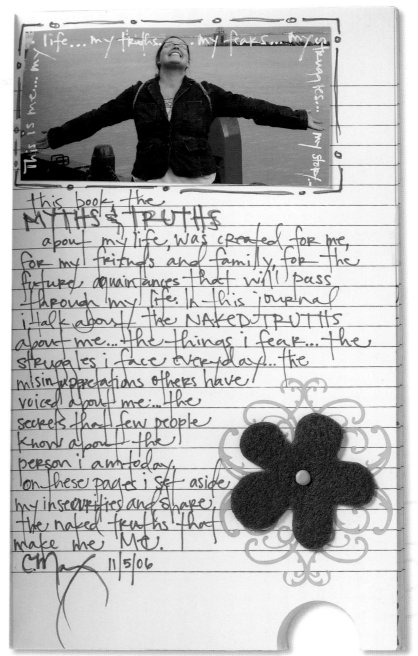

this book, the
MYTHS & TRUTHS
about my life, was created for me,
for my friends and family, for the
future acquaintances that will pass
through my life. In this journal
i talk about the NAKED TRUTHS
about me... the things i fear... the
struggles i face everyday... the
misinterpretations others have
voiced about me... the
secrets that few people
know about the
person i am today.
on these pages i set aside
my insecurities and share
the naked truths that
make me ME.
C.May   11/5/06

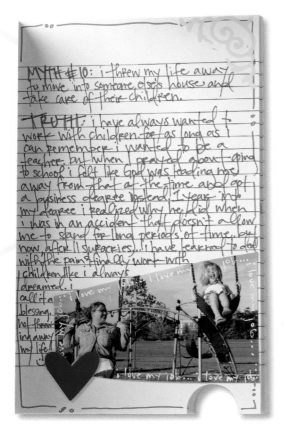

MYTH #10: i threw my life away to move into someone else's house and take care of their children.

TRUTH: i have always wanted to work with children. for as long as i can remember i wanted to be a teacher. but when i prayed about going to school i felt like God was leading me away from that. at the time and got a business degree instead. 1 year into my degree i realized why he did when i was in an accident that doesn't allow me to stand for long periods of time. by now after 11 surgeries... i have learned to deal with the pain. finally work with children like i always dreamed. i call it a blessing. they took away my life.

Only by much searching and mining are gold and diamonds obtained, and man can find every truth connected with his being if he will dig deep into the mine of his soul.

—JAMES ALLEN

What's Bottled Up Inside?

JOURNAL BY Sharon Soneff

PENT-UP EMOTIONS ARE ENORMOUSLY DESTRUCTIVE, AND NOT JUST TO THE PSYCHE. What is suppressed without expression the body generates into stress, which can result in ulcers, migraines, high blood pressure, and myriad somatic conditions. This project is a fun and crafty defense against this negative emotional repression. It also demonstrates a way of thinking about journaling beyond the traditional, bound book of lined pages. When the bottles of a favorite coffee drink (and its accompanying four-pack carrier) are covered in patterned papers, trims, and digitally designed labels, they become a whimsical representation of emotional struggles. More than approachable whimsicality, however, these bottles also offer practical functionality. Each of the four bottles is identified with one of four types, or "brands," of personal struggle. They then become receptacles for corresponding journaled entries. This literal displacing of "bottled-up" emotions, by putting them (via the journaling) into real bottles, enacts the releasing and freeing of negative stresses.

RIGHT An unorthodox and creative vehicle for journaling is sometimes just the fix for making the discipline feel less like a dry regimen. A journaling project such as this makes beginning the journey to healing inviting, approachable, and even fun!

A man who is master of himself can end a sorrow as easily as he can invent a pleasure. I don't want to be at the mercy of my emotions. I want to use them, to enjoy them, and to dominate them.

—OSCAR WILDE

RIGHT Bottles decorated and labeled for different areas of struggle are ready and waiting for journaling to be inserted whenever an emotional predicament arises.

BOTTOM A standard note pad and pen can be kept readily available for a quick vent or rant. Simply getting the emotions out of your system and onto a page is medicine for ailments of the spirit.

CREATIVE TIP

Scour your household pantry for unusual vessels to contain your journaling: pickle jars, coffee cans, and wide-mouthed bottles are all great candidates. These make great repositories for private thoughts.

Too Much On My Plate

JOURNAL BY **Deb Perry**

SOME HEALING JOURNALS ARE KEPT HIDDEN, STOWED IN DARK, PRIVATE DRAWERS for safe-keeping until the next appointed time for penning thoughts. This journal project is precisely the opposite: it is a decorative display piece. Granted, this is a rather unusual execution not common to most healing journals, but it is definitely one to be creatively explored. By setting our self-examinations onto a surface that can be seen and enjoyed often, its message (to examine priorities and live according to them) is more likely to be considered often, as well. Also, by finding metaphors for our lives in objects, we can apply natural laws and reasoning to extrapolate how such effects on an inanimate object might have similar effects on us. In seeing our life experience as a plate onto which, as the saying goes, we can get too much, we can visualize what the effects might be if we placed too much on it. If we cram too much on our plate or pile it too high, things fall off and get left behind, never to be tasted or appreciated. If we overload a paper plate (which might symbolize the self in a weak or frail state), it will actually cave in. Such a demonstration offers a moral to not take on too many unnecessary commitments when we find ourselves being stretched "paper thin." While it might be argued that approaching journaling in such a literal fashion is an oversimplification of difficult topics, it can also reasonably be asserted that bringing some abstract aspect of our lives into a physical, tangible expression can vividly spark an epiphany.

LEFT The form of this journal piece is a figural reminder that there are limits to our lives. Just like a plate with a set size, only so much can fit into it.

My Story

It began innocently—scrapbooking, that is. After all, who could blame me for wanting a creative outlet, a common bond with other artists, and the means to record memories for my family? But within a short time, scrapbooking became a vehicle for entering contests, gaining recognition, landing assignments for magazine and book publications, joining design teams, travel, and earning money. It was intoxicating. And just as quickly, too, I became obsessed with it—especially the recognition part. When I finally admitted what scrapbooking had turned into, I realized it was not something I was proud of—in fact, it was ugly. One day, I found myself letting many of my duties as wife, mother, sister, and daughter slip as I pursued the self-gratification of creating "lovely things." I remember putting the dishes away one night, and, in my mind, I saw the plate of my life full and running over. Unfortunately, the things that were piled on top were all out of order and wrong. This was my motivation for the plate journal. It's a visual reminder; it sits on my desk, so that I will remember that I am being called to continually find a balance, that I must always hold the priorities of my life up to this scrutiny. I discovered that, for me, it means putting this hobby at the bottom of the pile, not to be neglected, but not to be first anymore.

— Deb Perry

BOTTOM The circular pages of this journal are inset into the rim of a decoupaged plate. Hinges allow them to swing open and remind us of what should be given priority on the "plate" of our life experience.

There's a period of life when we swallow a knowledge of ourselves and it becomes either good or sour inside.

—PEARL BAILEY

Juggling Life

JOURNAL BY Sharon Soneff

MULTITASKING IS THE EARMARK OF OUR SOCIETY, in which the pressure to do it all and be it all is tremendous. For many, a great sense of obligation, an internal need to please others, or a fear of saying no can be the underlying reason for taking on heavy commitments and an overloaded schedule to match. Regardless of our logic or justification for overcommitting, the result can be tremendous emotional stress. Along with strong organizational skills, keeping a sense of humor and chronicling the lessons we've learned from our mistakes can be crucial to keeping us sane in the midst of a busy life. A creative journal such as this can be the ground for lighthearted but meaningful jottings. While keeping this journal might initially seem like just one more thing to add to the to-do list, in actuality, a few minutes of daily creative journaling can provide the resolve to deal with the balls we have to juggle on a given day, as well as the needed insight and wisdom to dodge incoming balls.

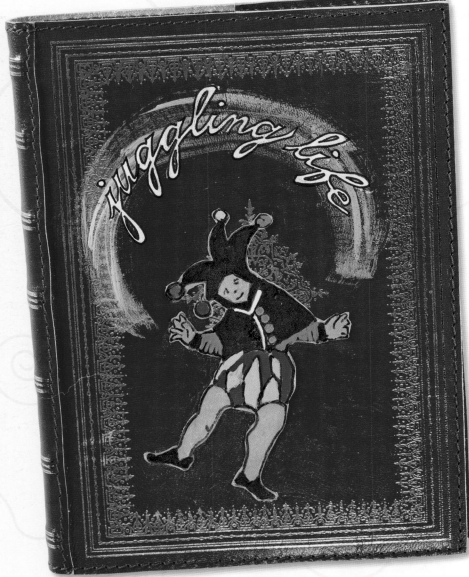

LEFT This royal-red leather journal, with gold foil–embossed detail, is the ground for further embellishment. A playful jester and title, applied to the face with gesso, acrylic paints, and opaque paint pens, introduce both the tone and subject matter of the journal.

CREATIVE TIP

Keep a full canister of pens at your disposal when journaling. Having various types of pens with different ink colors and thicknesses on hand provides opportunities for optimal expression. In this journal, opaque paint pens in various widths were used for the leather surface, while traditional ink pens were used on the paper pages of the interior. Permanent water-fast pens are needed when wet mediums such as watercolors will be layered over them. Broad widths and bright colors can visually scream out on one page, while fine-tipped pens and soft shades whisper on others.

BELOW The interior pages of this journal show the ongoing saga of the jester, this journal's central character. Cut into circles, Italian marbleized papers further the regal aesthetic and become the allegorical balls for this juggling act.

A fool often fails because he thinks what is difficult is easy.

—JOHN CHURTON COLLINS

What Wind and Water Cannot Wash Away

JOURNAL BY **Carol Banks**

WHEN NATURAL DISASTER BRINGS DESTRUCTION AND HAVOC INTO OUR LIVES, a journal can act as a shelter from the emotional storm that can accompany the literal storm. Structures and possessions can be ravaged by Mother Nature, whether in the form of a hurricane or tornado, earthquake or tsunami, fire or flood. Although the pages of the journal can be a place to lament these significant losses, there are things that can be salvaged from the aftermath of disaster. These often nontangible things are the true valuables in life. And never are they clung to more dearly, or with the greater appreciation, than when they are among the precious few things left intact.

Raked from the ruin and rubble, these untouchable riches can be mined to move towards health and healing. One of the hidden blessings of extreme loss is how it accentuates with vivid clarity what in our life is transitory and temporary and what is permanent and imperishable. Through journaling, we can transform times of tragedy into times of great clarity. Through journaling about catastrophe, we are given the rare chance to experience gratitude in a way that those who escape tragedy will never fully understand. This is the glorious treasure excavated from the darkest of days.

LEFT Ordinary corrugated cardboard is reclaimed to create the covers for this journal. Easily cut and scored, the cardboard is also distressed and peeled, foreshadowing the destruction of the hurricane spoken of within.

COme SiT a SPell

Spend a few moments in a place, beloved and treasured, that no longer exists except in the hearts of a lucky few...

Cherish the memories

ABOVE A photo of a beloved rocking chair captures the spirit of the genteel South and invites the journaler to linger and gather recollections of a bygone time.

Only after disaster can we be resurrected.

—CHUCK PALAHNIUK

WIND and WATER can

Memories of The old barn + tractor

The year Grandpa and Caitlin were inseparable

a little princess

heart + working man

Grandpa's babies

CHARACTER produced by HARD WORK

Strong arms noble heart Practical nature

Building family bonds

Precious Memories share

The patriotism which flew this flag each day in Kevin's honor and carefully removed it each night at dark.

ABOVE A collection of photos captures what life was like prior to the hurricane's destructive landfall. More important, though, are the thoughts penned onto the photos, which emphasize what absolutely nothing can wash away.

RIGHT Mediums, such as the textural paste seen here, lend movement and emotion to the page and contribute to visually telling the story. Working with tactile mediums is therapeutic, because it provides a way for us to release energy (and even frustration or anger) by applying it in various ways to a surface.

suddenly laid waste by Hurricane Rita

wash away

er in LOVE.

in 2
little boys
(and a
girl).

explore the pond ♡

arts hold these
memories close.

These things are ours forever. ♡

CREATIVE TIP

Textural effects can be added to your journals by using textural mediums and additives mixed with acrylic paints. You can buy acrylic texture gels containing crystal flakes, pumice, or flint. Or create your own textural mixtures by using sand, sawdust, or other inclusions as ingredients in your artful concoctions. For thicker effects, acrylic pastes are available; these can be brushed or sponged on or applied with a palette knife. You can scratch into or write on these mediums, embed items in them, or shape them into distinct or unusual formations. They can be left raw or painted over, if color is desired. The artistic outcome is unusual, expressive, and stirring.

My Story

My husband's grandfather owns a piece of land on the Louisiana coast, where he grew up. It was a place our family went to find a good helping of the peace of mind, body, and soul that belongs to an earlier generation. When Hurricane Rita hit the Gulf Coast, it was washed away in the blink of an eye.

For a long time, when I thought of Grand Chenier, I was filled with sorrow and the images of devastation: the house washed completely away, the cattle and their calves carried off by the storm surge, the smelly mud covering the once-fertile ground, proud trees crashed onto their sides or gouged by whipping telephone wires. I desperately needed a way to work through the loss and the vivid images of that storm, and it came in the form of this journal. Through creating it, I was able to remind myself that Grand Chenier is not what meets the eye when you go there today. It remains in our hearts what it always was before Rita came —a place of family togetherness, beauty, and old-fashioned simplicity. I close my eyes now and see those wonderful memories, which the mud and water cannot touch, and I dream of the day when the land is healed and it once again is a peaceful retreat.

—Carol Banks

Behind the Mask

JOURNAL BY **Sharon Soneff**

BELOW Card stock, cut to reflect the shape of the mask, constitutes the internal pages of this handmade journal. All components are hole-punched on the left and modestly bound with a single loop of black wire, making the book a one-of-a-kind artifact.

"PUTTING OUR BEST FACE FORWARD," TO CONVEY CONFIDENCE and competence, is a social tool most of us employ daily. And certainly, it is a perfectly acceptable way to operate in most of our social interactions with others. But sometimes, in so doing, the "best face" is actually a mask that covers what is really going on internally. Deceiving our closest friends and family—and, even worse, *ourselves* —is a dangerous masquerade. This journal provides a space in which we can perform a daily "face check" and work toward greater transparency in our relationships and increased honesty with ourselves. The cover of this lovely mask journal opens to reveal pages in which the things we hide can be identified and dealt with. Knowing our real state of internal affairs is at the core of self-repair.

Society is a masked ball, where everyone hides his real character, and reveals it by hiding.

—RALPH WALDO EMERSON

Contemplate all the creative options for making your own covers. The satin mask here is just one of infinite possibilities. A round paper plate is another simple concept for a whimsical cover and is easily punched and bound. Masonite or MDF are great surfaces on which to apply paint and mediums; they can be cut into unusual shapes and drilled for binding or lacing together with the internal pages.

TOP Black gesso, brushed onto many of the pages, creates a ground that echoes the black satin mask cover and also suggests the dark recesses of the heart that will be examined. Lovely upholstery trims and velvet ribbons encase and enclose these private divulgences.

Beneath an elegant masquerade

BOTTOM Each page explores a concealed emotion. Poetic admissions help the artist enlighten herself and push beyond the unlovely base feelings at issue.

doubt
questioning quelled

Good Medicine

JOURNAL BY **Sharon Soneff**

SICK AND HURTING PEOPLE MEDICATE THEMSELVES IN MANY WAYS. Sadly, drugs and alcohol are all too often the preference of some trying to cope with the difficulties of life. Numbing the pain in that way, however, simultaneously numbs passion, vision, motivation, and life, as well. These bad medicines also ultimately breed more difficulties—with relationships, career, and finances—which lead the victim to self-medicate even further, in response. And so the vicious downward spiral begins. Here, an art journal celebrates the alternative medicine of therapeutic art and the good medicines that can help the emotionally distraught. With an assortment of vintage ephemera, medical clip art, and mixed mediums, collages are composed to correspond with musings about the remedies for the soul.

LEFT With the charm of an old-time general store, this page's stringed tags inventory the positive remedies one can turn to for good mental health. Vintage prescriptions further the theme and are collaged to furnish an unusual ground for journaling.

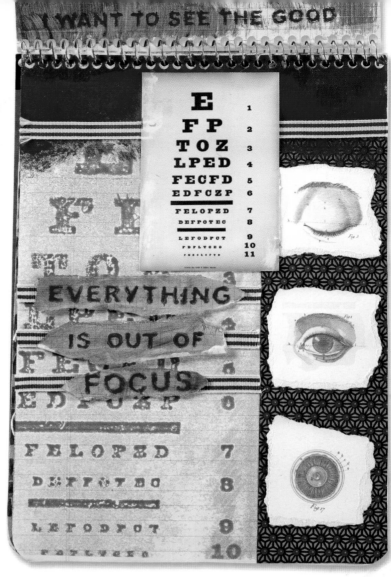

BOTTOM A found medical illustration of a heart provides a distinctive surface for journaling. The chambers and vessels of the heart offer places to position thoughts and observations about one's own heart-state.

TOP Continuing the vintage medical theme, an old eye chart is used to graphically offset the other elements of the page. Journaled thoughts are painted in deep crimson and pop out from the letters of the chart.

There is no medicine like hope, no incentive so great, and no tonic so powerful as expectation of something better tomorrow.

—ORISON SWETT MARDEN

Always in Our Hearts

JOURNAL BY **Jamie Harper**

SOME KINDS OF HEALING ARE BEST ACHIEVED CORPORATELY, such as in a group setting, where others who share the same plight can offer solace and comfort. Identifying with others who are experiencing difficulty in tandem with us provides the strength of numbers and the empowering knowledge that we are not alone in our hardship. These premises are the rudimentary foundations of group therapy. This can also be the rationale for undertaking a group journal. Whether it is a shared journal, a *circle journal* (one that is initiated by a group leader and then passed from one journal participant to the next, to each make their additions), or a corporate project, as seen here, the group experience can enhance healing. A difficult journey, such as moving through grief, is made easier with traveling companions who can help shoulder the load and offer a lifting hand.

This project provided an opportunity for this family of five to gather around the dining table over a central project. Young and old created something for, or about, the beloved paternal family figure who had passed on. Writing letters to him and drawing pictures for him soothed sad hearts and brought fond memories to mind. Not only did the healing occur in the safe harbor of home and among loved ones, the project gave the family unprecedented opportunities to grow closer. This journal is flexible in nature— it is intended to be revisited often and can be added to just as frequently. Another side benefit of the project, in addition to aiding the grief process: journal entries become tributes that form a legacy for this loved one.

BELOW A heart–shaped candy box is recycled for a new important duty. Instead of holding chocolates, it holds sweet sentiments of remembrance and expressions of grief over a lost loved one.

OPPOSITE Each journal entry is a unique expression of the family member who made it. Ribbons are stapled on the edges of each heart-shaped page for easier retrieval from the recesses of the box.

Think beyond the book concept when it comes to journaling. A recipe box filled with index cards could be your unique journal spot. So might an emptied tissue box, a tin container, a DVD case, or an unusual basket. Anything that can hold paper or inscribed words and artwork can be put into service as a journal.

Give sorrow words; the grief that does not speak whispers the o'er-fraught heart and bids it break.

—WILLIAM SHAKESPEARE

My Story

This creation has allowed so many feelings to be shared and tucked away. My father-in-law passed away two years ago; it was, and still is, devastating. Every once in a while, the kids would say something like, "I wish I could tell Grandpa ..." This thought came to me, to create a place where we could all keep our thoughts about him, write a letter to him, or just draw a picture. We all sat down and discussed the box and what it should be—the vote was unanimous: a heart, to keep him in our hearts. I made a box, and lots of papers to go inside, and told everyone to write or do whatever they wanted, whenever they wanted. I didn't know just how much this would help everyone express feelings that had been held inside. Every one of us, with the exception of Tyler, who is four, cried as we wrote. Emotions that had been buried now just flowed. My husband sobbed for hours, then hugged me and said thank-you, that he had really needed to take time to do that. He felt as though he was speaking with his dad again, which brought some healing. This project has brought us all closer as a family and strengthened our spiritual connection. I know that it is in the quiet, thoughtful moments that God can speak to us, and taking time to write from the heart has given us each a bit of heaven.

— Jamie Harper

Airing My Dirty Laundry

JOURNAL BY **Sharon Soneff**

MANY OF US GREW UP IN FAMILIES IN WHICH WE WERE TOLD THAT IT WAS NOT PROPER to "air your dirty laundry." The concept that, to preserve family dignity, dark and dirty secrets must be kept private was espoused for many generations. Sadly, this practice allows abuse to continue, enables addictions and vices to thrive, and isolates and silences those who most need support. Holding onto these dirty secrets only makes people feel bad about themselves. Conversely, functioning in truth and with transparency advocates airing out the soiled laundry of our soul. For, without getting it into the open, it will never be cleaned and renewed! A first step in refreshing our soul might be to create a journal, such as the one seen here. The next is to share our feelings with trusted friends and confidantes. Finally, as we become more comfortable with laying out our imperfect lives in plain view, then, and only then, are we able to help others in a profound way. Real family dignity comes from a place of honoring the truth and making reparation of offenses and wrongs. That is a reputation to be proud of.

LEFT Hand-painted calligraphic swirls symbolize the breezy, fresh renewal that this journal brings, as the "dirty laundry" that we stow away is brought out into the open spaces of the journal.

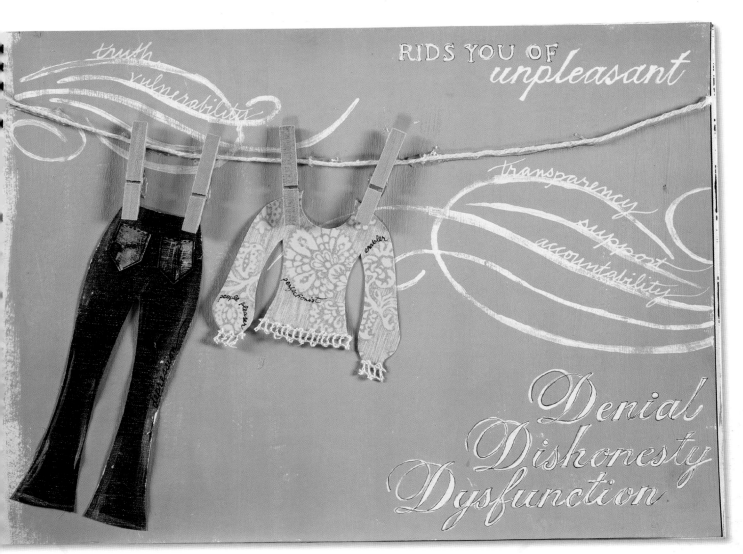

RIDS YOU OF *unpleasant*

truth
vulnerability

transparency
support
accountability

people pleaser *perfectionist* *enabler*

Denial
Dishonesty
Dysfunction

ABOVE The handmade clothes hanging from the journal's string clothesline are inscribed with statements of private turmoil. Here, the painted breezes of calligraphy state what it is needed to blow through our soiled situations: truth, vulnerability, transparency, support, and accountability.

Truth, like gold, is to be obtained not by its growth, but by washing away from it all that is not gold.

—LEO TOLSTOY

CREATIVE TIP

Not all journaling need be serious and somber. Taking a playful approach to crafting (such as engaging in paper-doll making or tactile finger painting, for instance) can encourage your inner child to come out and play. It can also help conjure up memories from your childhood and past and become a vehicle for restoration in a less-intimidating fashion. Do not feel that an art journal has to be "high art." An art journal is termed "art" because it is creative and expressive, and it can take countless forms!

Fear Not

JOURNAL BY Sharon Soneff

PHOBIAS CAN BE PARALYZING, but even common fears can become obstacles to growth and achievement. Facing, on paper, that which we fear and dread is a wonderful stride toward facing those same things in our daily lives. The journal page provides a virtual forum for practicing rational thought, which can later be conjured up when fears (and the irrational thoughts that accompany them) rear their ugly head. Coming to a better understanding of the fears that prevent us from enjoying and experiencing our lives can also be a catalyst for change and growth. Try using a journal to inventory those things that worry or even terrorize you. Then, register how your life might be improved if those worries and fears were removed. Finally, begin jotting down actions you can take to loosen and eventually free yourself from those confining chains. On paper, it's not such a scary thing to contemplate.

ABOVE A slender, wallet-size day planner is altered for use as a journal. Black gesso brushed onto the leather's surface primes the area for hand-lettering a title in metallic ink.

OPPOSITE On the left side of the journal, a silhouette drowns in her fear of water; opposite, a silhouette dives in freely, reaping the rewards that come with conquering that fear. Visually separating the fear on the left from the freedom on the right allows us to gain insight through comparison and contrast.

> Nothing in life is to be feared.
> It is only to be understood.
>
> —MARIE CURIE

My Story

I nearly drowned as a child. Had it not been for my older brother's strong arm, scooping me up, I probably would have sunk to that swimming pool's bottom. Swimming was just not something that my Midwest parents put a great deal of emphasis on, even after moving to Southern California. I did eventually learn to swim, but a lingering fear of the water still remained, and I still don't feel fully confident in the ocean, something that is a great disservice to me now, as I live in and rear my family in a seaside surf town. It has become important to me to overcome my water fears, because I want to wholly participate in our days spent at the beach and in the water sports that go with them. Although it is still a challenge, I have nurtured a desire to go ocean kayaking with my family to a degree that outweighs my apprehension of the sea, and I'm so glad that I have, because the experiences we share in the kayak are precious little adventures to me. The experience of journaling, identifying, and processing my fear of water has provided a pivotal lesson to me and an inspiration to conquer more of the fears that come between me and valuable experiences.

— Sharon Soneff

Evolution

JOURNALS BY Rebecca Brown

BECOMING UNBRIDLED FROM AN EMOTIONALLY PAINFUL PAST IS KEY to having a healthy, happy present. When life delivers a less-than-perfect start to our existence, we can become trapped in a mire of self-pity and snagged by negative patterns of thought over things that were largely or entirely out of our control. But what we do today, and how we proceed tomorrow, is entirely *in* our control. Journaling is a method to grab the reins of life. Self-monitoring through the journal helps to keep us from perpetuating the past or repeating that which could otherwise be happily laid to rest. Tracking the evolution of self, from a trail that began in a deep, dark valley through its ascension to the mountain top, is enormously empowering. The beauty and the prize of dedicating yourself to consistent, frequent journal-keeping is that the epiphanies of the moment are not missed, and every ascending, increasingly more enlightened step along the way is accounted for.

LEFT An array of journal entries shows the unfolding metamorphosis of thought, disposition, and emotional health. The rewards for having the courage to take a hard look at ourselves are a heart brimming with gratitude and a life transformed.

I am convinced that, except in a few extraordinary cases, one form or another of an unhappy childhood is essential to the formation of exceptional gifts.

—Thorton Wilder

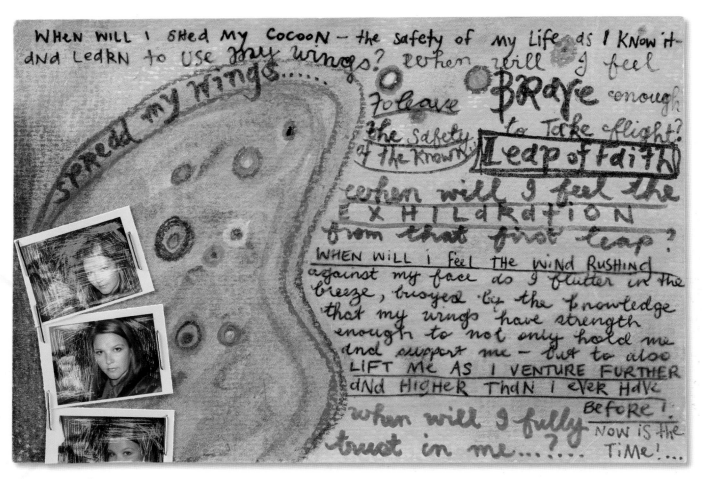

ABOVE A butterfly dynamically unfurls on the page. The artist's vibrant use of color encourages her to exemplify its soaring form in real life.

My Story

As a child, I thought that everyone else's life was similar to mine. I longed for the lives of my favorite TV show families but assumed that the dads were just being nice for the cameras.

As a teenager, I was filled with rage and pain, but I was conditioned to not express my emotions or give myself loving and healing. Growing up, my lack of trust in people led me to react to life through this curtain of anger and pain.

As an adult, I realized that, to find any measure of peace, I had to address these hurts, grieve for my lost childhood, and find a new way to live my life—not as a victim, but as a strong and loving woman who was able to overcome a harsh beginning and create a new life filled with love and family (worthy of any episode of the Brady Bunch!).

Writing poetry and creating art have been therapeutic and healing outlets for me. My art journal isn't about wallowing in the past; it's about learning from it and embracing it for the strengths it has forged in me. It is a story of living, conquering, and healing. It is my story, with my insights and my lessons learned. I wouldn't change my life for anything. It has made me too grateful, too empathetic, and too strong to ever wish for another. I feel my life, now—and it feels good!

—Rebecca Brown

BELOW Creative journaling is a technique for reconnecting to sensation when difficulty has caused you to disconnect from your emotions. These pages display the embracing of all feelings, whether they are painful or joyous, somber or blissful. When the emotional anesthesia wears off, the pain can be felt, but so can the euphoria.

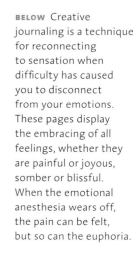

Journaling Worksheet 1

BY MINDY CALIGUIRE

Emotional Healing, Part One

Recovery groups have long espoused the adage, "You're only as sick as your secrets." And indeed, it often happens that great freedom emerges when we face our most difficult and troubling realities. Sometimes, that trouble represents a dark part of our history that needs to come to light. Sometimes, we just need to find a safe place in which to express the truth of what is going on *right now* in our lives.

The point is to let what's going on inside come out. To let what's true on the inside match, at least in this small corner of the world, what's going on outside.

Beyond the healing pages of an artistically designed journal, the things we now hold inside may eventually need to find their place in expression to a trusted friend, spiritual advisor, or to someone we've wounded. But, for now, the first step toward healing involves facing the truth, no matter how difficult that truth may be.

As you look over these questions, think of them as starter points. Some may resonate, others may not. Choose those that seem to resonate with you right now. Not all are essential for you to answer. Just one might provide the inspiration you need, as you start the process of creating your own healing journal.

Reacting to the Chapter:

● Which of the sample journals in this chapter spoke to you most? Why?

● Whose story did you most identify with? What did you find in common?

● Which journal, if any, most directly connects to your life right now?

● Which relates most to a past season of your life?

Reacting to Your Life:

● When you think of the idea of "Peace," what immediately comes to mind? What colors? What images? What places or people or objects seem most peaceful to you?

● Write three or more sentences about a time in your life when you experienced peace in a relatively strong way.

● What represents the greatest barrier to peace for you these days?

● What emotions have been sources of turmoil for you lately?

● What emotions are you most likely to avoid feeling or to "stuff"? What factors have influenced this area of life the most? If your truest concerns were visible to others, how might they be characterized? Bold colors? Hazy and vague images? Or colors drawn outside the lines?

● When you are not "feeling" your emotions, what are you most likely to do with them? In what way has this indirect way of handling emotions helped the situation? In what way, if any, has it hurt the situation?

A Piece of Me Is Missing

JOURNAL BY **Carol Banks**

FOR THOSE SERVING IN THE MILITARY, AND FOR THOSE AWAITING THEIR SAFE RETURN, the stress can be great. Against the noble backdrop of duty and honor, these military families undergo a good deal of emotional trauma in their daily lives. A journal can be a way to cope with the emotional gamut of the military experience, from the dignity, pride, and discipline to the fear, horror, sorrow, and stress. The portability of a journal means that almost anyone—even a soldier half a world away—can carry it almost anywhere. The wounds of war are manifold, and, although not every soldier returns with visible scars, scars can nonetheless be present. Pouring thoughts onto the page is like a salve for these invisible wounds.

Equally in need of a coping journal might be the soldier's family, which is pressed to manage agonizing feelings— fear and apprehension, for example, which accompany the constant awareness of a loved one's mortality, and loneliness, when a person who is an integral part of your daily life is absent. In a journal, both the harrowing and tedious are given the same regard, the blank page an open invitation to anything needing to be unloaded and a sanctuary from political agendas or decorum.

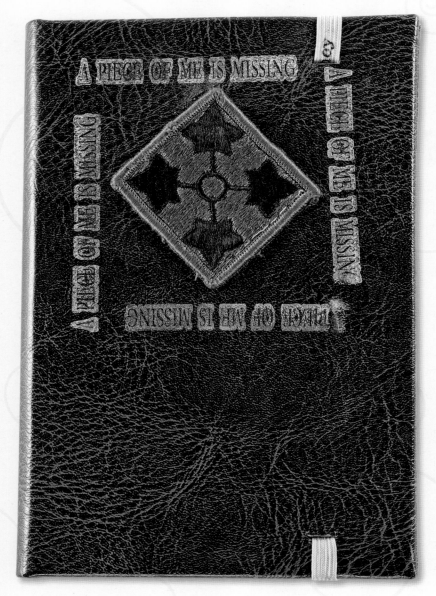

LEFT A combat patch on the cover of this handsome leather journal symbolizes the deployment of the artist's husband with the Fourth Infantry Division. The emblematic patch is framed by a repeating stamped phrase revealing the artist's emotions.

TOP Tell-it-like-it-is journaling is flanked by pertinent photos. This style of journaling, which covers every emotion (good, bad, and ugly), offers an effective outlet for a daily buildup of pressures.

BOTTOM Newspaper headlines offer both graphic interest and a visual statement of wartime stresses. The artist uses colored markers to override the world news with statements that hit a little closer to home.

Tis the soldier's life to have their balmy slumbers waked with strife.

—WILLIAM SHAKESPEARE

SO THANKFUL FOR

e-mail

The Internet techs in Taji, Iraq, for giving Kevin a link home.

The power of prayer and a loving Lord ✝

proud of Kevin

being so

long, hot baths

Strangers who said, "Thank you for your sacrifice."

STRENGTH from ABOVE

Weekly phone calls

AMBIEN

...pletely devoted to each other

my parents, for being there.

A trustworthy MECHANIC

A loving, strong and s... ...table marriage, com...

The book "I Married Adventure" by Luci Swindoll

Yahoo Instant Messenger

Little Caesars Hot and Ready $5 Pizza

My new job teaching sweet, cute 3-year-olds

Scrapbooking: expressive outlet, social activity, and temporary escape.

ProFlowers.com

Chocolate

123-SCRAP

My friends at

Letting the tears flow sometimes

Beloved family and friends all over the country, praying.

Silly movies ☺ and laughter

Prayer was like a transporter — I felt closer to him.

buddy

Melissa, my battle

Our resilient, adaptable kids

HUGS

Bob Babcock's bi-weekly 4th Infantry Division updates

Uncle Sammy, who can help to fix a lawn mower over the phone.

MY SANITY SAVERS

WELCOME H♥ME DADDY!

We are proud of you

Weeping may last for the night, but a shout of joy comes in the morning. Ps. 30:5

WELC...

TOP LEFT A hand-drawn grid of boxes is a clever way to encapsulate journaling and photos. As demonstrated in this journal, the big and little things that make up the safety net of your life can be treated as a visual network or tiling of words. Think of it as a word grid with which to gird your emotions.

BOTTOM LEFT Even a simple quote helps bring wisdom and healing. When a scripture is placed alongside photos of this soldier's return, the result is wisdom and revelation that heals. If a proverb or precept speaks to you, include it in your journal. If a quotation helps you cope, it is part of your healing story.

CREATIVE TIP

Just as the newspaper clippings were used to create a telling background, other paper scraps can be recycled for an exalted use. Classified ads, phone book pages, and maps are provocative base papers. A flea market find of vintage wallpaper might serve as a lovely ground for meaningful journaling or collage. Even ordinary household items, such as dryer sheets and paper towels, can be layered with paint and medium, to make an unusual groundscape.

My Story

Being a military wife has its benefits, and I am proud that my husband serves as a chaplain in the U.S. Army. But it also has more than its share of challenges. Unquestionably, one of the biggest of these is deployments. To me, this small journal packs a wallop; it is a receptacle for all the emotions I stored up inside during our first taste of deployment, when my husband spent a year in Iraq. Just making the journal was cathartic, allowing me to take some of the turmoil I was feeling and get it outside of myself, in a visual format. All the newspaper clippings on the first pages—all the negativity and tension of war that is dumped into the media on a daily basis—came from a single issue of the newspaper. Cutting and chopping all those bits of headlines and words, sticking them to the paper, and covering them over with glue and paint was so therapeutic. Writing over the chaos of clippings, I let loose with all the other noise in my life: the children's tension, my own fear and loneliness, the words and images that fogged my world. Stepping back and looking at it gave me a more objective point of view, helping me realize that I could never make it through this by myself and that, thankfully, I am not alone on this journey. On the next page, I rejoice in the things that bring some sense of order to the chaos, the resources that help me through. There was a multitude of blessings, from the "big" things, such as my strong personal faith and our family's devotion to one another, to the "little" things, such as Yahoo! Messenger and take-out pizza. Just looking at that page makes me smile, because it is a powerful reminder that even in the middle of deployment, a military wife is not alone.

—Carol Banks

Love Letters

JOURNAL BY **Karan Simoni**

IN THE PURSUIT OF LOVE AND COMPANIONSHIP, it is nearly impossible to avoid encountering heartache along the way. Love is Mecca, the destination for the pilgrimage that every heart must make. Even so, the breakups, betrayal, infidelities, and divorce that are often part of the search for intimacy can be disheartening.

The journal can act as a teacher and guide, with a curriculum designed specifically for you and based on your experiences. When you record and reflect on the past, you create a lesson book for your future. Becoming a student of yourself allows a self-love to emerge, a love that can then be offered to another. When it seems that love comes and goes, a journal is constant. When it seems that no one is reliable, the journal is. It is from this solidity that stable relationships are born.

And, even when the earth moves beneath you, you will find your footing, always ready to step courageously and passionately forward.

'Tis better to have loved and lost than never to have loved at all.

—ALFRED, LORD TENNYSON

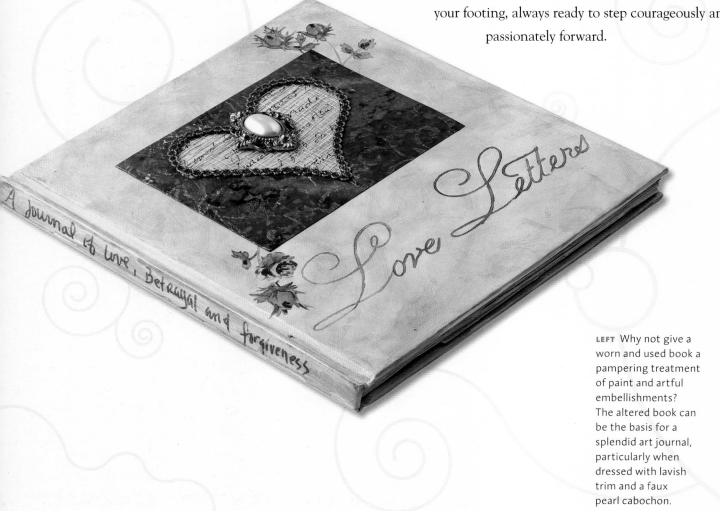

LEFT Why not give a worn and used book a pampering treatment of paint and artful embellishments? The altered book can be the basis for a splendid art journal, particularly when dressed with lavish trim and a faux pearl cabochon.

My Story

This is my story of love—lost and found and lost again—and how I found my way back to loving, even more deeply and strongly, because of the pain. It happened because I was able to see past the hurt to the gifts I received in the process. Healing truly begins when you focus on the gifts and the positive things you take away from a negative situation. It is through this process that you learn to love yourself, when you can be thankful, even for the painful times, seeing them as lessons that take you to a new, clearer place of understanding. That is where love really lives.

I created this journal for me and for my children. I want them to know that it is okay to fail several times, as long as you learn and grow from the experience. I want them to see that I never gave up on my dream of love.

—Karan Simoni

BOTTOM Part affirmation and part proclamation, journal entries combine with color and form to create a montage in which learning to love one's self becomes the basis for loving others.

TOP Each page of an altered book receives a brushy application of gesso. The gesso creates a ground for many treatments, from penned sentiments to collage executions. Collected magazine ads and editorial snippets can be composed to create your own story of imagery and text.

Going in Circles

JOURNAL BY **Marilyn Healey**

RAISING AND REARING A LARGE FAMILY IS AN UNDERTAKING WITH HUGE REWARD. But often that which is enormously satisfying is also enormously exhausting. The requirements of being a caregiver can leave one feeling dull headed and emotionally emaciated. And while children can provide so much love and delight, filling a home with humor, wonder, innocence, and liveliness, the reality is those very same energetic little ones may leave us drained. This is especially true when the mix includes the unique and widespread demands of both a toddler and/or a teen. But every family consists of unique developing people with unique demands and schedules. Addressing every need and every demand of your little ones cannot be done at its optimum without you too meeting your own needs. The journal is there to help make that happen. Concurrently, a case of the "mommy guilts" can be cured. Realizing the magnitude of your mom-job is easily done when you begin to list out the numerous things you accomplish on any given day. Try writing your job description. Chances are you will give yourself a huge pat on the back and a sizeable promotion.

LEFT An assemblage of circles, from rounded layers of paint and paper to the filigree frame adhered to the vintage book's face, perpetuates this mother's feeling of constantly going in circles. Also, a repetition of fours (as seen in the domino, the chipboard disk, and the vintage photo) is used to figuratively represent the artist's own four children.

they are eating my brain!

GRIMM'S FAIRY TALES

Let your emotions take cues from color. If dark, heavy hues help you unleash what is emotionally bound, grab deep-colored materials to work with. Conversely, if light shades and bright colors help to elevate your mood and encourage a more hopeful outlook, then let those tones dictate your artistic expression. When you let your emotions be the artist that determines color and material, both dark and light can heal.

ABOVE The altered book of fairy tales becomes home to a narrative of a different kind. With drips of walnut ink and blotches of sky blue paint, this art journal is transformed into the quirky catharsis of an artful mother in search of her wits and perhaps a little wisdom.

Sometimes the strength of motherhood is greater than natural laws.

—BARBARA KINGSLOVER

*To keep a lamp burning we
have to keep putting oil in it.*

—MOTHER TERESA

Sometimes
I wanna
hide.

many a question was asked

I was driving to the store and I was grump
PH was grumpy at home and the kids h
been naughty. nobody was happy...Fe
discouraged. I thought about this
later I wondered if other families f
happier th...
than I...

How do you get a teenager

not just parents being mean to him?

My Story

We always said we wanted four kids. With the first two, it was wonderful, most of the time. It was fulfilling. With the addition of a third, we decided that three was really enough. Secretly, I knew we weren't done. I put it out of my mind, to think about again in a few years. But, Heavenly Father knew he had to step in, or we would never get around to having that fourth child. Number four was a surprise—our Bonus Baby, as we sometimes refer to her. We had just moved, and our lives were still in disarray, when we found out Amelia was coming. Being pregnant was very hard on me physically, and I wasn't able to be the organized person I usually was. To this day, I am still trying to get "moved in" all the way. Seems four kids is sometimes more than I can handle. The fulfillment I once felt being a mother was gone as I struggled to care for my family and still perform all the other tasks that life requires. I felt like I was always playing catch-up. I was miserable in my crazy life.

Now I always fear that, in putting my true feelings "out there," I might be judged unfairly. I am crazy about my kids. I love them. But I am having a hard time feeling happy about my job as a mom. The house can get very messy and unorganized, and I was frustrated by the messy house and the kids fighting, crying, being rowdy, and not following the rules.

My artwork is truly what keeps me going; it's the one thing that I enjoy and look forward to—the bright spot in my life. Making a book a place in which I can record my feelings, thoughts, and concerns turned out to be a lot more beneficial than I had expected. I don't know why, but I have felt less discouraged lately and have been a better mom. My book makes me wonder if my feelings are justified, or if I am just being a baby and feeling sorry for myself. Sometimes it does let me know when I am feeling sorry for myself.

My "Mom book" is not finished and it probably won't be for a long time. I plan to continue to fill it with whatever thoughts I need to add and with things I have learned.

—Marilyn Healey

Reflections

JOURNAL BY Janelle Simons

THERE IS NEVER A CHANCE FOR SATISFACTION AND HAPPINESS when we set a perfect (and unrealistic) ideal as our criterion of self. When we compare that perfect standard to our real life, disillusionment is the certain outcome. But when the image we strive for is that of strength and beauty of character, achieved only through an imperfect existence, our whole perception is changed. We no longer need to strive for the unattainable but, instead, garner beauty and fashion strength from the imperfection of our daily lives.

Facing trials with courage, and looking them in the face, is what makes us strong. A journal can be a mirror for doing just that. At first, what we see staring back at us may not be attractive. But only that looking glass of truth can give us the view needed to create change. Adjustments in our perception require the fine tuning that can be learned through consistent journaling practices, shifting negative thoughts into positive ones, and exchanging a dismal, dark lens for one that is clear and enlightened.

BELOW Broken pieces of mirror grace the cover of this spiral-bound journal and illustrate how perfectionism broke and shattered this artist. The patterned papers and leafy *ribbonrie* add a Victorian garden appeal, showing us that, even in the midst of brokenness, we can be made beautiful.

This is the very perfection of a man, to find out his own imperfection.

—SAINT AUGUSTINE

TOP A found vintage image pasted into the pages of the journal perfectly demonstrates the change in perspective being experienced. From a dark lens to a clear one, a shift occurs in the way that life and all its challenges can be viewed.

BOTTOM The artist shows her intention to get truth from merely being understood to where it is embraced by the heart with bold paint in simple shapes and a colorful array of stickers arcing across the pages, from the head to the heart.

My Story

A hormonal disease brought a lot of changes into my life that left me weakened and depressed. Longing for peace, I began to search my heart. I realized that this bump in the road did not fit into the plans I had made for my life. I began to see that, to beat the depression, I had to come to the understanding that life wasn't meant to be perfect. It is life's imperfections that build our character. I had to shift my vision and learn to love and accept myself as I was intended to be. As my vision changed, the depression lifted. I see now that striving for perfection never strengthens anyone, it only makes us feel inadequate. When we pass through life's struggles and victories and learn from them, it gives others hope. Journaling helped me to reflect on all that God had done in me through this season, how much my vision had changed, and how much more peace I now have. It allowed me to see how my spirit has been strengthened by facing the trials of life.

— Janelle Simons

Once They Were Happy

JOURNAL BY Emily Falconbridge

WHEN DIVORCE DIVIDES A COUPLE, THOSE WHO LOVE THEM ARE RIPPED APART, TOO. A divorce is not just the dissolution of vows and marital commitment, it is also a disintegration of the couple's dreams for the future. Those who had imagined themselves a part of that future, especially children, can feel that their dreams have been dashed, as well.

When a marital tear rends the fabric of an entire family, all who were a part of the family quilt must participate in its mending and patching. The art journal serves as an opportunity to pose questions that we are afraid to ask, to release ourselves and others of blame, and to acquaint ourselves with this couple as individuals, apart from the roles they played in their marriage. When we find forgiveness and understanding, the seams of the family can be re-sewn. The family quilt might not look quite the same, but we can find unique beauty in the new pattern that manifests.

LEFT Sometimes our journaling sends us back in time. Using the mediums of our childhood, such as chubby crayons and trays of rainbow-colored watercolors, can allow our memories and emotions to heal.

However often a marriage is dissolved, it remains indissoluble. Real divorce, the divorce of the heart and nerve and fiber, does not exist, since there is no divorce from memory.

—VIRGILIA PETERSON

CREATIVE TIP

Put a little elbow grease into your emotional angst. In so doing, you lend an interesting distress to your paper. Use sandpaper, scouring pads, or wire brushes on paper to yield unrepeatable textures. Scratching up photos is a hands-on method for adding artful character and interest and exerting emotional energy, at the same time.

My Story

I love that my journal can be a place for me to put the happy and the not-so-happy. It's a place to put feelings and emotions and hopes and dreams, a reason for me to work through the things that I have going on in my life, a chance to spend the time sitting and thinking and getting inside my own head, while I swirl paint or stitch with my sewing machine. My parents divorced just a few years ago, when I was expecting my first baby. It was a weird time for me. My mother gave me their wedding album, as she no longer wanted it, and I feel so much sadness looking at the pictures of them with so many possibilities laying ahead. Having the chance to think and journal about the parts of my life that bring me sadness helps me work through my emotions and also tell the full story, which my kids might one day want to read.

—Emily Falconbridge

LEFT Spatial relationships and divisions can be illustrative in a journal. The wedding day photo cut in half is compelling, as is the red stitching that unifies it again.

I Was Just a Little Girl

JOURNAL BY **Emily Falconbridge**

REPRESSION IS A TOOL OF THE PSYCHE TO BLOCK SOMETHING TOO TERRIBLE TO CONTEND WITH. When an innocent child is the victim of a grievous act, her psyche can act to protect her, concealing these horrific things from her conscious mind. Often, however, the memory eventually creeps back to the surface of consciousness at a later date, at which time this revelation requires some earnest processing. The art journal can be a nonthreatening, non-judgmental recipient of disclosures when these admissions are still raw and strange. Its pages are a safe shelter for the most vulnerable. Sometimes, the signs of abuse are present, even before the abuse is fully realized by the victim—journaling can actually unleash the repression. Beckoned by the child's play of art, the guarded memories can emerge in its sheltered spaces.

RIGHT Revisiting the past may be necessary for healing. Old photos allow you to observe with compassion the child you once were. As you become eyewitness and onlooker to your own experiences, the commentary that materializes will lend an empathy that you can then extend to yourself.

CREATIVE TIP

Art journals are intended to house quick-work, pieces that do not require much artistic debate. However, this does not mean that you cannot make multiple visits to the same page. On your initial venture, you might paint your background and ink some thoughts. The next time you visit the page, you add more forms, this time scrawled in paint. Another visit might consist of adding artful and whimsical details, such as the sewn ruffle seen here, or maybe buttons and ribbons. Layers added in progressive journaling sessions can culminate in art and understanding that are both rich and deep.

So, like a forgotten fire, a childhood can always flare up again within us.

—GASTON BACHELARD

My Story

When I look at pictures of me as a little girl, it makes me sad to think of the hurt that was inside. I want to go back and protect that little girl, to stop those teenage boys, to tell someone what was happening. I want to cuddle that little girl and make everything better. It was sad for me to create this first-ever page about the abuse that occurred when I was a child. It was sad, but it was also empowering—it helped me to realize how strong I have become, how far I have come in healing, and how little it affects my life now. It is part of who I am, it helped to shape me as a person. I think, because of my experiences, I am more compassionate, more understanding, and more aware than I would otherwise have been. By leaving this out of my journals and scrapbooks, I would be fooling myself and others about who I have become.

—Emily Falconbridge

LEFT An art journal can reveal how a past abuse can manifest itself in our present life. In the healing journal process, we can glean a wisdom from our past and nurture hope for what lies ahead. Reconciliation with the past can bring healing for the future.

health and healing for the emotions   **59**

Grace Under Pressure

JOURNAL BY **Sharon Soneff**

TAKING AN OBJECTIVE LOOK AT THE PREDICAMENTS INTO WHICH WE GET OURSELVES can be both healthy and humorous. This book of comical scenarios is an insightful, creative method of self-examination. The juxtaposition of materials is a playful display of profound revelations. Just as literature and theater effectively use these devices, so can art; the sublime use of the absurd begs the audience (in this case, the journaler) to ask questions with fascinating answers. On a stage of collage, the coquettish victims almost compel you to call out to them. And in so doing, you find your own answers. Why put so much energy into keeping up appearances, when that energy could be put to better use protecting yourself from disaster? Why be concerned with entertaining and delighting others when you are about to be swallowed up whole? Why not shed a heavy gown, when being weighted with the splendid attire means being trapped? Why be coy and preoccupied with poise when you should be screaming for help? The absurdities of these circumstances help us see our own falsehoods and foolishness.

BELOW LEFT Although the interior pages are speedy expressions in collage, the journal as a whole is created with some attention to setting the stage. A graphically designed cover is adhered to a modest spiral notebook. Wrapping the coiled binding in sumptuous flocked paper elevates it to a grand state.

BELOW RIGHT Glue is precisely brushed onto the spider web photo and dusted with iridescent art glitter. The fantastical scenes are fashioned to always be just a bit more lovely than they are macabre.

My Story

Being a perfect lady, keeping my composure even in a high-pressure situation, is highly important to me. Taught at a young age to behave with manners and to concern myself with propriety, my preoccupation with being a woman of grace and elegance has been an asset to me socially. But when decorum gets in the way of being real, it can be detrimental. Appearing to have it all together can be intimidating to others—and it's really a bunch of smoke and mirrors half the time, anyway. I have also come to realize that conveying that I'm doing fine, when I'm in the middle of some real personal pain or turmoil, prevents my friends and family from giving me the love and help they want to offer. Grace and manners are still important to me, but authenticity and transparency share equal importance. The art journal helps me project my genuine self to others.

—Sharon Soneff

TOP French fashion illustrations embody ladylike grace, which seems utterly preposterous with the tornado whipping its fury behind. A few choice words snipped from a vintage dictionary add clarification.

BOTTOM An unlikely scene elicits thoughtful participation in the haps and mishaps of such a lady.

CREATIVE TIP

Sewing notions, such as thread, trim, snaps, buttons, and clasps, add tactile dimension to a journal page. Accoutrements such as these can help you illustrate your story and personify your mood.

By "guts," I mean grace under pressure.
—ERNEST HEMINGWAY

My Hope Is Peace

JOURNAL BY Tammy Kay

BEING THE TARGET OF PREJUDICE IS EMOTIONALLY INJURIOUS. Regardless of the reason for being slighted—race, gender, appearance, religion—without a loving support system, strong faith, tenacious reason, and an outlet such as journaling, it would be easy to become embittered. But bitterness and resentment does not forward a prejudice-free society. Love does. Peace does. Knowledge does. Conviction does. These are the things we want to cultivate internally and pass on to our future generations.

Within a journal, hurts can be freely expressed and released. In exchange, we can gain the strength to compose powerful words that urge us toward acts of tolerance, equanimity, goodwill, forgiveness, and benevolence. Developing strong opinions through journaling can lead to actions that heal in the community. Along the way, not only does our own heart heal, but so begins the mending of our world.

RIGHT A beautiful photo of this biracial couple's hands is the centerpiece for conveying unity, love, and peace in this journal entry. It is also the inspirational springboard for the journaling.

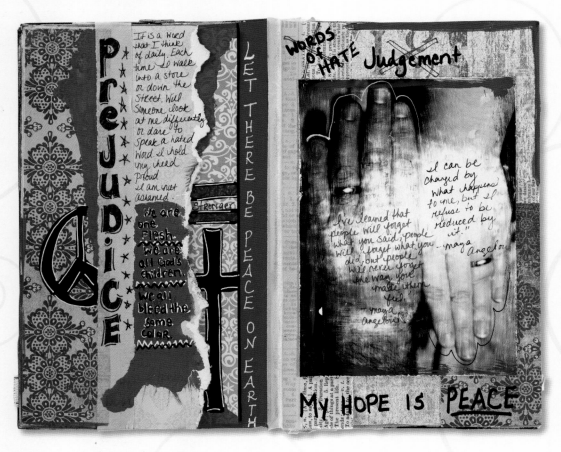

One day our descendants will think it incredible that we paid so much attention to things like the amount of melanin in our skin or the shape of our eyes or our gender instead of the unique identities of each of us as complex human beings.

—FRANKLIN THOMAS

Unlike a scrapbook, in which the use of archival adhesives is important, a journal can employ nonarchival methods, such as staples and masking tape, to secure photos. This provides an enormous amount of artistic freedom.

BELOW The artist's children provide her with the motivation to inspire change in a world where prejudice still exists. Helping society become more informed and evolved also provides a catalyst for change. By identifying the things that move us to action, we can become people of word and deed.

My Story

I have thought so many times about all the hate in this world and just felt helpless. Living in a small town, I stand with a mere handful of others who share my view of marriage. I realize that I could become bitter. I could blame the people who point fingers and stare, for their prejudice and for allowing it to continue. When I sat down to work on my journal entry, I took all the pain and tried to express it in words. I asked myself, "Why? Why am I hurt? Why do I care what others think?" The answer was simple: my children. They are my reason. They are why my story is so very important. They are why my anger was turned into words of hope. My hope lies in them and in telling my story. I could not see what I hoped for, inside me. Writing it down made it real. I left my mark. I cannot change the world, but I can take a piece of myself and share my life—through artwork, through my creative process.

—Tammy Kay

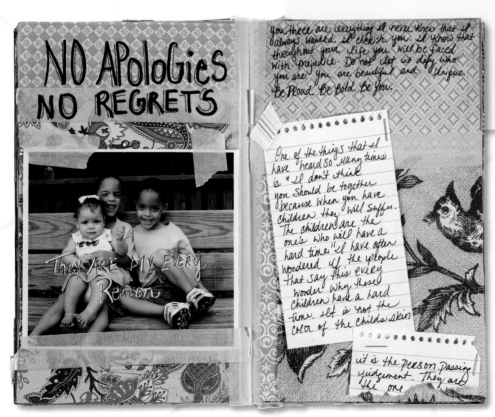

Now More Than Ever

JOURNAL BY **Liz Eaton**

JUST LIKE A BODY THAT SITS MOTIONLESS, A LIFE THAT IS NOT IN MOTION CAN ATROPHY. In the same way a still pool of water can grow stagnant and murky, so can a static life become stale and even putrid. But what is the countermeasure to such a fate?

A forward-moving life requires internal motivation. Initiative is born out of desire, and desire can be generated by the stimulating practice of journal-keeping. Being productive includes more than writing task lists, however—it also requires writing about why those things are on the list, and then examining where we want the task list to take us. Gaining the energy to move means finding out what fuels us.

BELOW Stamped and dated, an art journal can be a milestone or marker. Frequent, thoughtful marking of time can lead to a more conscious life.

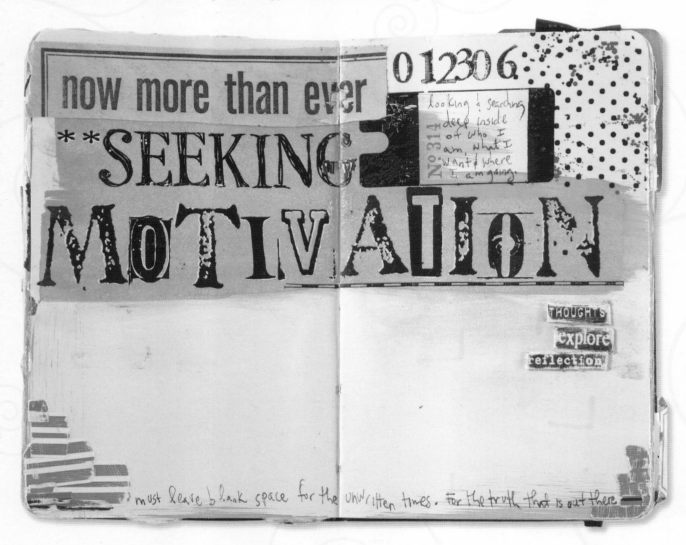

People often say that motivation doesn't last.
Well, neither does bathing—that's why we recommend it daily.

—ZIG ZIGLAR

CREATIVE TIP

Various charts and diagrams can be used for creative illustration. What about using a Venn diagram of overlapping circles to find common territory between two emotionally charged decisions? Why not log the peaks and valleys of your moods on a graph? A bar or pie chart can break down information in a visually clear way. And since charts, graphs, and diagrams are visual devices, they are a perfect fit for visually rich creative journals.

My Story

I started this journal to battle my ongoing struggle to stay focused and motivated on a daily basis. I have never been one to procrastinate or sit around and twiddle my thumbs, but I do feel that I get distracted and sidetracked from what needs to be accomplished. This journal is a great reminder of the daily things I need to do, to stay on task. In the past two years, I have discovered that working for myself, alone at home, is harder than I ever thought it would be. It's so easy to get distracted by the things that are necessary to run a smooth, clean household. Sometimes, I think it would be much easier to go to an office or to work for someone else, but then I remember how much freedom and creativity I have because I work for myself. That is when I usually find myself pulling out my journal and creating a new page, as a reminder to take action now, to not let another day pass. I mean, really, "If not now, when?"

—Liz Eaton

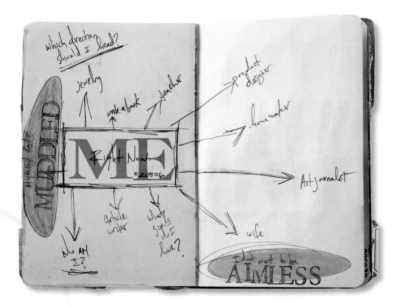

TOP Creating a "mind map," or flow chart, is a great way to clarify thoughts. Determining direction and aim on paper helps us make our mark in life.

BOTTOM The artist used masks to create the word "action" and the box around it. When black spray paint is applied and the masks removed, the result is high impact.

Money Matters

JOURNAL BY **Sharon Soneff**

FINANCES—THE MANAGING OF THEM OR THE LACK THEREOF—precipitate emotional apprehension. Budgeting, even when done with consummate self-discipline, can put strain on us. A self-imposed debt trap can be dispiriting and seem insurmountable. Even investing and saving a surplus of cash can be cause for consternation. Money matters, it would seem, are also matters of the heart. Frequently, the disposition of our finances affects the disposition of our heart; other times, it is the heart that affects decisions regarding our funds, but, truly, they are tied to each other.

Fortunately, the pages of the art journal are available to address every topic, even those of a fiscal nature. Examining the reasons behind expenditures, both the highly impulsive and the heavily considered, merits your time and energy. Tracking our financial footsteps (and missteps) through a creative map, a visual scale, or an artful collage can lead to a revelation about where our revenue goes. For the visual person, this could be the precise demonstration needed for clarity. When we employ artful reflection, we can learn to better align the priorities of our pocketbook with the priorities of our heart.

BELOW A set of envelopes, each with a distinct artful execution and message, is kept together by a single book ring. Journaling entries, slipped inside each of the envelopes, elaborate on the money-related topics labeling the outsides.

Make all you can, save all you can, give all you can.

—JOHN WESLEY

My Story

With my husband and I both being self-employed, we really have enjoyed the flexibilities our careers have afforded us, allowing us to be the masters of our own schedules and giving us more time with our kids. But we also have endured the immense emotional stresses of not getting the dependable paycheck every two weeks. No company benefits, no pension fund, no health insurance—self-employment definitely has its downside, as well. Learning to generate revenue and make it work for us is something at which we have sometimes flagrantly failed and other times glowingly succeeded. Discovering how to thrive in a feast-or-famine profession has been trial and error, and these financially driven emotional stresses have even fueled fights between us, at times. But all these twenty years later, what we've really come to own is our intangible wealth. This commonly shared realization that we have things that money can't begin to buy leaves us feeling enormously blessed. We have also seen that laying out our finances on paper can reveal some surprising findings. It has helped us stabilize our income and satisfy our craving for consistency. We hope we have learned some lessons about money management along the way, too, but more important, we have learned that our money and our professions do not define us.

—Sharon Soneff

I Never Knew How Much

JOURNAL BY **Emily Falconbridge**

SOME THINGS PLAY SO HEAVY A PART IN COMPRISING WHO WE ARE that removing or altering them is markedly felt. Like baking powder in a cake recipe, some components are not really appreciated until they are tampered with or omitted.

Sometimes, when our lives feel entirely off-kilter, it is not until we pause for examination that we realize that we have inadvertently lost or even purposefully removed something integral to us. The art journal is a great diagnostic tool for asking, "What have I changed?" or "Why was that so important to me?" Whether you move on, to create a new recipe for your life, or restore the ratios that were comfortable and familiar to you is really your choice. In either case, the art journal can assist you as you seek to restore or reinvent yourself. It is certainly within your power to do either!

RIGHT Remnants, such as a ripped memo pad and a piece of masking tape, become the background and foreground for journaling. A rubber stamp, designed with lines for the purposes of focused journaling, is used in the composition.

Life consists not simply in what heredity and environment do to us but in what we make out of what they do to us.

—HARRY EMERSON FOSDICK

Starkly beautiful
and captivatingly
simple, the minimalism
of this journal combines
comfort and consolation
with affirmation.

CREATIVE TIP

A creative exercise to try in your art journaling exploits is to alternate between sparse minimalism and lush abundance of word and form. One day, challenge yourself to use all form and no words. Another day, allow yourself to run rampant with language. Neither is the right or wrong way to approach a creative journal, but in practicing both approaches, you may find that one clicks with you and provides an expression that is particularly medicinal to the makeup of your soul's health and healing.

My Story

After twenty-seven years of living in a beautiful old house nestled in the bushland of western Australia, my husband, daughter, and I moved to Los Angeles, to a small apartment by the side of a fourteen-lane freeway! It was the complete antithesis of where we had come from and was quite a culture shock. I have always loved being so near to nature but didn't realize what an impact it had on my soul and mental health until it was taken away from me. To not have my own patch of outdoors to lie in the grass with the sun shining down on me, to breathe fresh air and to listen to the quiet—being apart from all that ate away at me. After several months, I had a little art corner built and finally felt inspired enough to start creating again. Being able to journal and tell the stories behind my pictures helps me and also helps my little girl in this transition.

In the middle of this transition, I also realized that, sometimes, you have to just make a reminder to yourself that things will be okay. Leaving my family, friends, a lot of my belongings, and all of my roots behind, to move halfway around the world, to a place in which I didn't know a single person was a huge deal for me. But we felt it was a journey we had to take. As we were packing up to leave our precious house in Australia, I made this blue journal page. I didn't quite believe it at the time, but I told myself everything would all be all right. The page stayed up on the wall for quite some time in our new apartment. When everything was finally okay, it went into my journal.

—Emily Falconbridge

Enjoy the Journey

JOURNAL BY **Rachel Denbow**

TAKING ON A NEW ROLE, OR JUST ANTICIPATING IT, CAN CAUSE EMOTIONAL DURESS—even when it is something we desired and felt entirely excited about. Such is in the case for many people when they embark on parenthood. Contemplating the great responsibility of caring for another life can be worrisome, to say the least. But clutching onto the worries can cause you to miss the joy in the journey. Releasing your ruminations onto the page and accepting the post of mother can be done, in part, with creative expression. The journal can also help you discover your parenting style, be a disciple of the accomplished mothers around you, and become a student of your child, learning his or her every like and dislike. This journaling approach can propel you toward finding your comfortable and confident stride as a mom.

My Story

As for many mothers, my days are full of diapers, drool, and a constant awareness of someone else. There are moments when the word "overwhelmed" seems appropriate. The anxiety of doing irreparable damage to my child has faded with the experience of his resilience and has been replaced with a sense of purpose. I am a mother. I have a great responsibility to teach my son about the world and his role in it. To be the best mother, I have to make time for myself.

I notice how much he has grown when I stop to look at pictures of him when he was younger. Not only do I want to document the early months of our new son through journaling, I want to use art as a way to validate my life experiences. When I make a piece about an event, as trivial as it seems, it becomes a marker in time. This helps me to see everyday moments as special times with my son. I have rattles in my purse, pureed carrots on our kitchen floor, and bed head until his second nap of the day, but someday, I am going to wish life was just like this again.

—Rachel Denbow

Trust yourself.
You know more than you think you do.
—BENJAMIN SPOCK

Aspire

JOURNAL BY Tammy Kushnir

OBSESSIONS THAT CRIPPLE THINKING AND FUNCTION CAN BE COMMITTED TO A JOURNALED PAGE, in which their repetitiveness, instead of burying us, can be buried in a medium. By temporarily captivating a mind and gripping its attention, art can be a healthy diversion from other obsessions that engross us. It has been shown that, for many plagued by addictive or obsessive personalities, a successful strategy is to replace unhealthy addictions and obsessions with positive ones. By offering the mind a surrogate, such as creative journaling, it is able to free itself from the clutches of disabling habits.

The book arts provide a platform for expressing in form and phrase things that are sometimes unutterable. Here, myriad mixed mediums—paint, wax, and vintage photos—create an unfolding picture of progress. Thoughts born out of struggle are lightly penciled into the medium, becoming whispers secondary to the profound art of passage. While the book's first pages convey a colorless and dismal place, the latter pages express an emergence from the darkness and into a state of health, a sunny, buoyant place to which we can aspire.

Your aspirations are your possibilities.

—SAMUEL JOHNSON

LEFT Enigmatically beautiful, this altered book is shrouded in layers of thick, white medium. A frail, wispy feather, tacked down with medical tape, acts as the cover's focal point.

TOP LEFT The sketched nude torso conveys the artist's vulnerability. In a kneeling and prayerful position, this identity cries out for help from the imperfect angels in her life.

TOP RIGHT The vintage photo of the bare female torso parallels a desire to bare the soul. Surrounded by dark, clouded applications of medium, handwritten confessions move mysteriously in and out of the artistic murkiness.

BOTTOM Another vintage photo, of a subject whose face is placidly content, not as gloomy and sullen as the previous subjects, is the centerpiece here. A hoped-for happy ending shines through with sunny yellow paint and offers the encouragement to continue to aspire.

My Story

OCD (Obsessive-Compulsive Disorder) has been a part of my life for as long as I can remember. I didn't realize, until I was older, that my fears and obsessions went all the way back to the beginning. As I grew older, the OCD symptoms morphed from one to another, ranging from getting things "just right" to hand washing and finally to obsessing that I may have hurt, not just the people closest to me, but complete strangers, as well, by actions that often occurred only in my head. Some days would feel like dreams in which vivid thinking confused my reality and left me wondering what was real and what was only in my imagination. It wasn't until after the birth of my first child that I got serious about therapy and medicine. A bad previous experience with medication left me fearful of trying something new. But there was no other option. I was going to lose my beautiful baby and husband if I didn't get help, so I did. The medicine worked, thankfully, but finding a good therapist took a long time. In the years since starting therapy and a medication regimen, I began to desire the process of creating altered and handmade books. More recently, I felt courageous enough to display personal phrases inside the books, a type of journaling created to be shared with the many others who also suffer in silence. At first, I wondered if people would think me insane to be admitting to such strange and confusing problems. A part of my OCD crept out, prompting me to ask myself if admitting such horrible feelings out loud and in view of others might ruin me. The opposite happened. I began to find it therapeutic, not just for me, but also for others who contacted me and let me know that I was making a difference to them, as well. Although I am far from being "cured," I am finally at a place where I can say, concerning my life and obsessions, that I am uncertain what may or may not have happened in my past and am uncertain about what may happen in my future. To many, this might seem a bit unusual, but in the world of an OCD sufferer, to be able to say those words with confidence is magical.

—Tammy Kushnir

CREATIVE TIP

The feathers and dried flowers in this journal are more than mere objects d' art. Natural items can embody the qualities that tell your story. A leaf, a broken twig, or a shell might become a touchstone to emotion.

BELOW Adhered together and clasped at the corners, multiple pages can be carved into, to create niches. A vintage photo and tiny cork-topped bottle are recessed and framed in this stratum.

Journaling Worksheet 2

BY MINDY CALIGUIRE

Emotional Healing, Part Two

Losses have a funny way about them. Whether they sneak up on us without a moment's notice, or they happen invisibly and catch up to us later in life, we all face losses. And that funny way about them is hardly funny at all—they really hurt. A lot. We lose loved ones, we lose our sense of control, we lose our way in life, we lose our independence, we lose relationships, financial security, and even, tragically, our innocence. And while it would seem obvious that losses in life are inevitable, the irony of spiritual growth is that often our losses can lead us to a deeper reality. They can lead us to a place where our souls can be touched.

But to experience life and growth, our losses must be seen, felt, acknowledged, and grieved over, if necessary. In a way, they must be honored, even the smallest of the. A wise friend once advised, "What you grieve, you keep." Irony.

Perhaps a next step in your spiritual journey will involve honoring just such a loss in your own life. As you honor it, you can also receive the gift of moving into the future, not only having been wounded by the loss but also having been opened to a healing touch along the way. Maybe you already know what has touched your soul through the loss—maybe you will not know until you go through the process.

Reacting to the chapter:

- What examples of loss can you identify among the journals in this chapter?

- What about these journals do you imagine offered or expressed a gift of healing to the artist?

- Which of these journals impacted you most intensely? Why?

Reacting to Your life:

- Make a list of five or ten significant losses that you have experienced (even light-hearted ones, such as the loss of your independence when you became a new mom).

- Pick one to work on. If you were to represent that loss using images, colors, shapes, and textures, which would you choose? Why?

- Now, write a few sentences about how that experience shaped or is shaping you, for better or for worse. Have you become more fearful? More careful? Do you have a new perspective on life? Finish the following sentence, if it help:

   Because of that loss, I _____ or since that time, I _____ .

- What help did you receive along the way, and how can you represent this in your journal? Who were the people who brought help and guidance? What quotes inspired (or still inspire) you?

- What do you sense you need as you move forward? Write a few sentences about that, being as specific as you can about what you need and how it would help you.

- What are your highest hopes for the future? Again, jot down the images, colors, shapes, and textures that represent those hopes.

Health and Healing for the Body

Finding Comfort in the Midst of Physical Challenges

ALTHOUGH A CREATIVE JOURNAL CANNOT CURE ALL THAT AILS YOUR BODY, what it *can* do is act as an important aspect of treatment for physical sickness and unhealthiness.

The creative journal can move us toward healthy habits and cement our resolutions to treat our bodies well. Its pages can serve to record a plan for fitness, document medical test results, and track conversations with our trainer or physician. It can mobilize us during a difficult time, when we need to rally all our strength and courage to fight disease. The same journal might be a confidante when we receive a difficult diagnosis and are plagued by doubts, denial, anger, or sadness. And yes, it can act as a dependable, perpetual balm to chronic pain.

The body has enormous aptitude for self-repair and healing but it tends only to work at its best when we do the necessary internal work. Devoid of negative side effects, creative journaling has only benefits to offer—the benefits of resolve, resilience, wisdom, and inner strength. Our body can draw on all these inner resources to create physical verve and energy.

When journaling for a physical result, aim to incorporate these helpful aspects:

- *Integrate tactile mediums.* The more tactile the medium, the more physically connected to your journal you become. Assert your muscle and your brain, to achieve that mind/body connection. Get your fingers involved, not only in writing and illustrating, but in raw ways, as well—smudging charcoal, rubbing transfers, or carving niches, for example. Be physically invested in your journal and in your life.

- *Be specific in characterizing your physical complaints and goals.* Specificity not only helps clarify thought, it can bring clarity to your functional plan of action. Regardless of whether you act on your plan alone, or in conjunction with physicians, the information will prove invaluable.

Natural forces within us are the true healers of disease.

—HIPPOCRATES

- *Have faith that the internal work labored over in journaling will manifest itself in a physical way.* Because this aspect is the least tangible, it is the most difficult, but it truly is the most important. Science supports the belief that faith and hope can be determining factors in equipping your body to face its most difficult challenges. So, step out into the unknown; your journal will supply the company and the comfort in unknown territory.

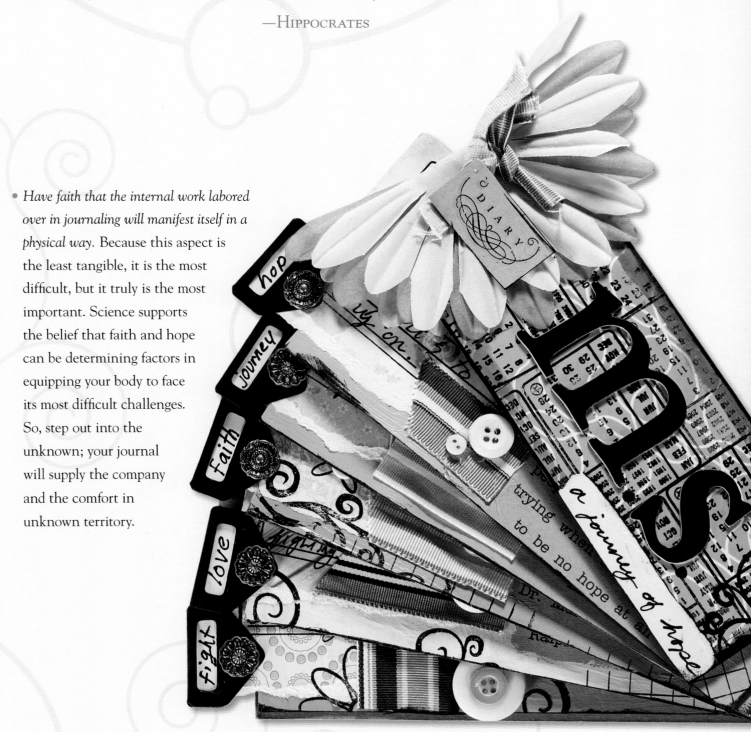

Mirror, Mirror

JOURNAL BY **Allison Schubert**

NONE OF US ARE WITHOUT SKELETONS IN OUR CLOSETS. But, for some, staving off their bony grip is a lifelong battle. Eating disorders are among these insidious physical plagues, requiring keen vigilance from those who suffer from them. Participating daily in a creative journal can help provide the vigilance needed for lifelong recovery. The journal acts as a looking glass—through the reflecting process, we can see ourselves, our progresses, and our regressions—giving us the means to make needed adjustments along the way. The honest and accountable self-monitoring that journaling requires helps to keep you from falling back on old attitudes and habits and prevent those skeletons from pulling you back into the dark retreats of isolating illness.

In the exposed pages of the creative journal, the skeletons lose their power over us. We no longer have to fear and heed them; instead, we make those skeletons do our bidding. That which we are conquering need not be shameful or hidden away, it can be something over which we take pride in our mastery.

RIGHT This journal's cover, with its many layers and varied materials, is both beguiling and complex. A self-portrait photo is printed onto reflective silver stock and mounted beneath a gilded frame. Obscuring the photo is a stamped and glazed skeleton figure, which sets the stage for the journal's pages.

RIGHT This page, devoted to understanding one's skewed and distorted perspective, also lends a considerate ear to the cries and hollers from the soul. In the photograph, crystals mimic tears falling from the artist's eye.

If you can't get rid of the skeleton in your closet, you'd best teach it to dance.

—George Bernard Shaw

little one... I pray you'll never know this struggle
this is my greatest fear.

I thought by now I would have recovered
But your life has chosen a different course

You are still too young to understand
But the time for your realizations is coming soon.

What will I tell you?
How do I explain or justify
My need to be so thin?

My love for you is everlasting
I will continue to fight this disease
I can face anything as long as I have you

You are the love of my life
The reason I have not already given up

You are my legacy
My hope and salvation for a better tomorrow.
"BellaDonna"

Natural Beauty

LETTER
to my daughter

ABOVE The spaces of a journal offer an opportunity to speak to someone else—in the form of a letter, for example. This enormously useful format allows you to express love, extend compassion, pass on wisdom, or even ask for forgiveness. Here, the artist grapples with how to explain her eating disorder to her daughter, but it also focuses on how her daughter is an inspiration to live in health.

My Story

My recovery has been a long, complicated, and difficult struggle. Anorexia is like a shadow that follows you everywhere you go, and it is so easy to slip back into that lifestyle. Putting my feelings down on paper offered many rewards. Going through anorexia was devastating and painful—it's a part of my life that I don't want to forget. It's a place I don't want to go back to, either. But, if I remember, I can tell my story to my daughter and to others. I have also realized, by doing this entry, how strong I really am because I did survive. I survived the rehab, the diet pill overdoses, the laxative abuse, and my body's shutting down. I survived, and I am stronger today.

—Allison Schubert

LEFT The skeleton, whose first appearance on the journal's cover seemed menacing, reappears here in a much more relaxed stance and is now donning angelic wings. Further signifying the change in health, another photo of the artist's eye sports a twinkling star, instead of tears.

Insomniac

JOURNAL BY Shimelle Laine

For most of us, the dark of night provides the sweetness of slumber and the rest that our mind and body requires to be healthy and alert when the sun rises the next day. But the setting sun can cause distress to those who desire sleep but cannot find it. Tossing and turning on the mattress that should otherwise be a platform for a full night's sleep can be pure torment. Finding the illusive cure for insomnia can be equally as torturous. What can a creative journal do for such an affliction? Discharging thoughts and worries onto paper can provide peace of mind and a state of internal quietness that might be just what's needed to predicate sleep. Silencing the voices in your head can be as simple as committing them to the page.

The body and mind both benefit from a predictable schedule; including in your nightly pre-bedtime ritual a period of art journaling can help ready you for sleep. The rhythmic movements of writing and painting can also have a soothing effect. And if sleep evades you, just knowing that your journal is waiting for you in those lonely wee hours can prompt a shift in how those nighttime hours are perceived. This change in perception can cause changes in the body as well, creating less stress. Let the creative journal be an antidote to stress—a restful mind can only aid a restless body.

LEFT A sinister figure, screen-printed on this moleskin journal, personifies the menacing problem of insomnia. (See Resources, page 125, for the Toothfaeries screen print).

TOP Scale of imagery and type can convey the tone of the journaling. Here a boldly stamped statement virtually shouts out the relief and joy that progress brings.

BOTTOM Even the journal's hue encourages a sleepy mood. A groundscape of dreamy blue paint, suggesting a dusky night sky, is perfect for journaling about sleep issues.

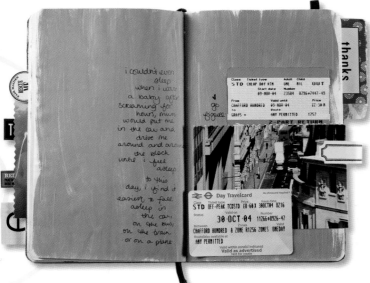

The worst thing in the world is to try to sleep and not to.

—F. Scott Fitzgerald

My Story

I have suffered from insomnia all my life, even when I didn't know what it was. As a child, I would wait for everyone else to go to sleep, then start wandering around the house looking for something to do, something that got me into serious mischief more than once. I eventually found ways to work my insomnia into my regular life. I went to school early and stayed late. I worked the last shift on my first job and didn't mind being the last person out the door. At university, it was perfectly acceptable to be a night owl; everyone thought I was studying until the wee hours of the morning. Even when my first teaching job required being on a train by 6 AM, I would have been working until three or four in the morning. There's always something else to do, right?

This journal was created in retrospect; I use it to express my fears about insomnia. Although I finally put it to rest, I often worry that my insomnia will return. From time to time, I add to this journal to help me make sense of my anxiety about it and to remind me not to panic. I don't know what a medical professional might say about keeping a journal as a safety net, but it's a process that works for me, and I'm glad the book has so many pages, to keep all my thoughts in one place.

—Shimelle Laine

Strange and Fabulous

JOURNAL BY Rachel Denbow

Huge physical transformations, even when attributed to a joyous cause, such as pregnancy, can be alarming. Experiencing radical hormone shifts and unfamiliar physical symptoms and characteristics can shake even the most stable woman. Therapeutic art and journaling can accompany you as you venture into these unknown territories. As your body becomes an exaggerated form, brimming with the life within, the journal can parallel the experience with aggrandized forms and lively entries. Worries about labor and the baby's health, questions about yourself in this new lifelong role as mother, can all be addressed in the pages between the covers of the journal. The journal can also be a platform to celebrate the mysterious and the wondrous, as your body works hard to make the miracle of life within. Just as your baby has a safe womb for healthy development, you too can have your own womblike environment in the secure and protected pages of the artist's journal. There, your health can be fostered in artfully created pages, summoning strength, conjuring courage, and evoking wisdom as you walk into the unknown regions of your life.

BELOW Emotive and honest journaling fills the expansive painted ground. Both successes and failures are penned with freeform candor.

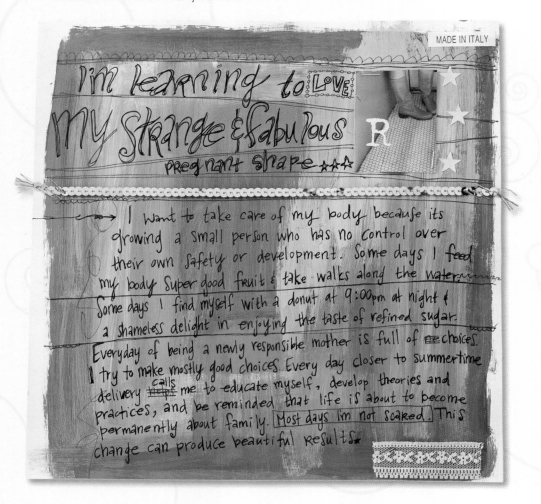

OPPOSITE A circle segmented by slices of color and texture serves up clever spots in which inscriptions can be made. Here, the artist appoints attributes she hopes motherhood will foster in her.

I still marvel at the miracle of birth—how every part of my body was made ready for that moment.

—Judith MacNutt

My Story

I fought my pregnant shape throughout all three trimesters. I wanted to keep things under control, so I walked, took a birthing class, and ate healthy food. I struggled with embracing my curves, because I felt like they were disappearing into one large shape. (I waddled long before I noticed myself in a storefront window.) It was the first time in a long time that I had to prepare for something important without seeing any benefits.

The sacrifices I had to make were small. I lost my taste for coffee and didn't mind cutting back on tuna fish, and when the only thing that took care of first trimester nausea was Coca-Cola, some sacrifices became optional. Needless to say, I wasn't enjoying the healthy glow, the thicker hair, and the attention from strangers as much as some said I would. With my hormones riding shotgun to my reason, I needed a way to keep things in perspective. Journaling helped me clear my thoughts and remember what a beautiful thing was growing inside me. Using color and 3-D objects along with my words not only eased my mind but allowed me to create something memorable. After all, your first pregnancy only happens once.

—Rachel Denbow

Conquer the World

JOURNAL BY **Danea Burleson**

A PHYSICAL CHALLENGE THAT LEAVES YOUR BODY IN A CRIPPLED STATE need not cripple your spirit or your life. The unique and figural journal shown here describes the way the artist chose to live the life she desires and not let physical limitations dictate the limitations of her dreams. Whether you employ artful, imaginative play or contemplative narratives of self, journaling allows you to travel outside the confines and restraints of your human shell. The journal can move you past mental obstacles, through emotional challenges, and beyond physical constraints. What's more, the journal is adaptable to any environment, from the bedside table to the wheelchair. Even when contending with crippled hands, you can explore alternate methods of expression. Finger-painting (which is less about motor dexterity than it is about dragging and pushing a tactile medium) is an option that offers the same expression of other mediums. Adaptive computer software is another means of fashioning an art journal. Regardless of the method you need to use, indulging in the creative journal practice will provide recreational, and, even more important, rehabilitative benefits.

BELOW Inventive journaling is slipped into the sole of a high-heeled shoe, which is decked out with artful execution. This journal typifies how we can live expressively and vicariously, through figural and symbolic pieces.

To strive with difficulties, and to conquer them, is the highest human felicity.

—DR. SAMUEL JOHNSON

CREATIVE TIP

An object of your affection can form a foundation for your art journal. Let the pocket of a worn pair of your favorite jeans store a spiral-bound, flip notebook for journaling. Use a beloved scarf or bandana to slipcover an album or book. An earring that has lost its mate can be fashioned into a clasp or bookmark. Recycling something you love into a journal will in turn foster love for the journaling.

My Story

Growing up with rheumatoid arthritis was trying, but most of the time, to me, it was just the norm—I didn't know anything different. I wasn't a shy child, and, although I was insecure about the way the disease made me look, I never let on. I didn't care so much that my hands didn't look normal, but, for some reason, I was afraid to show my feet. I never wore flip-flops, or open-toed shoes. I would admire pretty sandals from afar and keep my socks on at all times. It wasn't until two years ago, at the age of 30, that I realized how silly I was to worry about what other people thought. One morning, I braved wearing a pair of flip-flops, my oddly shaped, crippled toes exposed in all their glory. Out with my husband in public, my anxiety was high, but —lo and behold—no one even noticed! I felt free. Although I do get stares at times, I just politely smile. I have a great love of shoes, but, although I can now wear flip-flops, these crippled feet will not endure heels. I am OK with that. I have come to accept my fate of flat, comfy shoes, but that doesn't mean I can't admire those glamorous and feminine heels. Freeing myself from my foot fears opened my eyes to other possibilities. One day, at the local thrift store, I came across a pair of pretty black pumps. They weren't my size, but I had to have them. By transforming those heels into an altered journal, I found a way to have my shoes, and enjoy them too. Pain-free.

—Danea Burleson

Beauty Against the Beast

JOURNAL BY Genine Devlahovich

CANCER CAN BE AN AGGRESSIVE DISEASE, RAVAGING YOUR BODY. Although it might attempt to steal your beauty and your femininity, ultimately, it cannot. For, the real beauty you possess—the charms and grace of your womanhood—are impermeable. There is so much cancer cannot begin to affect or touch, and the mixed-media journal seen here celebrates that. Incorporating mammogram X-rays and medical test results into collage pieces transforms the fearsome into a thing of beauty. Curvy shapes in paper-art form make a home to celebrate the real essence of female strength and attractiveness. After all, what is more beautiful than a woman who allows her inner beauty to shine forth? What is more beautiful than a woman who, in the end, subdues a frightening beast? There truly is nothing more beautiful or inspiring. Your beast may be cancer, or it may be diabetes. It may be alcoholism, or it may be depression. Whatever creature tries to impose devastation in your life, foster and nurture formidable beauty in the pages of your art journal, and, in the end, your enduring and everlasting beauty will remain unscathed.

CREATIVE TIP

In the realm of healing journals, less is not more. Be generous in proffering your thoughts and emotions. Any and every little thing that bears significance to you is worth including. What results is a rich, magnificent montage, in which every detail works in accord to bring meaning to you.

My Story

Everything seemingly came down on me on the day I was told that the shadow on my mammogram was indeed cancer, not only in my breast but also in the lymph nodes under my arm. When you hear news like this, your brain sort of glitches and fails to compute. It's like you're in a tunnel, and the doctor is far, far away, at the other end. I could barely hear him tell me that "your cancer is in advanced stages, and you will need a mastectomy along with sixteen weeks of chemo and six weeks of radiation." I was frozen; I didn't murmur a word. I was so glad that my husband could ask questions on my behalf. It is the kind of experience that no one should face alone. Throughout that whole day, I felt as if I had had no other time before, as if I were floating—almost "out of my body."

After my surgery, I felt helpless, not because I had lost my breast, but because I had cancer and only I could save myself! It really got me thinking about how we are born alone (unless you have a twin) and will die alone. Everyone has their time to die, but it seemed mine was approaching rapidly. I stayed awake many nights, wondering whether I would see my oldest daughter graduate high school, or whether my husband would be the one to see my son off to his first day of kindergarten.

I think it was God's way of putting a speed bump in my life. Prior to my diagnosis, I really took things for granted, as my life sped by. I now know that every day with which I am blessed needs to be embraced.

"Thankful" isn't really a word you associate with cancer, but I am thankful for all the wonderful people I have met on this journey of highs and lows, an occasional U-turn, and a lot of rest stops! "Cancer" is a strong word, but I have found my inner strength through it, and journaling helped me uncover that strength. Cancer is responsible for making me stronger in body and in spirit.

—Genine Devlahovich

TOP Hand-scripted journaling is as lovely to look at as it is inspiring. A familiar and comforting handwritten mantra for cancer patients acts as a beautiful reminder of the disease's limitations.

BOTTOM A rich montage of imagery captures the artist's mix of emotions occurring on the day of diagnosis. The literal and the symbolic create full and loaded expression.

My Burning Desire

JOURNAL BY **Jamie Harper**

MASTERING YOUR BEHAVIOR FOR THE SAKE OF PHYSICAL HEALTH REQUIRES GREAT DESIRE, self-discipline, and commitment. But, although the requirements are great, so is the reward. When setting out to regain control of your health, an art journal can help you keep your eye on the prize and strengthen the desire and discipline you need to claim that prize. The pages of the art journal can be a creative training ground for the mind, so that you can in turn train your body. One of the draws of hiring a professional personal trainer is that they can offer motivation, pacing, and monitoring. But when the *self* is appointed in the role of personal trainer, a journal becomes nearly imperative to provide those services. If, in your journal, you can create a fire to fuel you, your burning desire will not be extinguished. When ignited by this intense passion, you are sure to gain great health and healing.

BELOW A vintage book cut carefully into the shape of blazing flames is a strong visual statement that echoes the book's theme and sets the tone for internal entries.

A strong passion…will insure success, for the desire of the end will point out the means.

—WILLAM HAZLITT

My Story

I have struggled with weight most of my life. Although
I have had a constant burning desire to lose weight, it
has not been matched by my follow-through. After
struggling through the years, I finally made a promise
to myself that I would get healthy. The weight was not
the issue; I wanted to get healthy and stay healthy. But
where would I start? When the road to health is long,
with no instant gratification, how would I get motivated?
This journal was my answer. After writing in it, I was
able to see what was stopping me. I used my journal to
learn about my behaviors and what would work for me.
It was amazing how simple the process really became,
in the end—not the work, but the decision to just do it.
And, it is a lifetime commitment, because I'm doing it for
health, not weight. So, it is ironic that I lost the weight
by pushing the weight aside.

—Jamie Harper

LEFT Splayed open,
the book's unique
silhouette invites
journaling of a
passionate and
sometimes
graphic nature.

Balance

JOURNAL BY Emily Falconbridge

FINDING THE PATH TO OPTIMUM HEALTH IS REALLY A VOYAGE OF DISCOVERY. Blazing new trails in the realms of shopping, cooking, and eating can take us into foreign terrain. This can be both exciting and overwhelming, because there are so many health cultures to sample. Often, discovering what clicks with our life and body is achieved through experimentation. Because our bodies are as unique as our psyches, we may have to contend with uncommon allergies or intolerances. In the end, however, genuine health and happiness is achieved by avoiding extremes. An art journal can help you define your health objectives and document your experiments with new health practices and your body's response to them. The art journal can also provide objectivity, so you don't find yourself teetering precariously away from the ideal and stable core of balanced well-being. As you find solid footing in the topography of your healthy new lifestyle, you will also find the energy and joy that comes from such equilibrium.

*The best and safest thing is to keep
a balance in your life, acknowledge
the great powers around us and in us.
If you can do that, and live that way,
you are really a wise man.*

—EURIPIDES

BELOW Exploring and pursuing a dietary regimen inspired the artist to create this page. Taking cues from the yin and yang principles of a macrobiotic lifestyle, the page balances cool and hot hues.

My Story

Three years ago, when I began studying macrobiotics, my world changed. I now think differently and know so much more about what I put into my body. My journey is constantly changing, as I struggle to find the time, balance, and discipline to eat in the way that I want to, but I am learning along the way and am grateful for my experiences and growth. This journal page reminds me that my journey is ongoing, to do my best and continue on to health and happiness!

—Emily Falconbridge

CREATIVE TIP

Thin your paint to a drippy consistency, and allow splotches of color to be dropped from your brush. The pattern and size of the splotches you create are dictated by the amount of medium loaded onto the bristles and how high the brush is held above the paper. These unpredictable, irregular dots can enhance your journaling entries with capricious texture and form.

Love Renewed

JOURNAL AND POETRY BY Mary Zakrajsek

WHEN LIGHTNING STRIKES NOT ONCE, BUT TWICE, OR EVEN MULTIPLE TIMES, succumbing to anger along with the disease can seem only natural. But, through raw and honest journaling, these emotions can bloom into vivid outward expression, allowing the spirit to soar above and triumph over disease. When we are challenged by terminal illness, processing thoughts about death and eternity become forced onto us. Yet, what seems an assassination of our future can also present us with an opportunity to focus on our eternal legacy. As this artist demonstrates, illness, even that which leaves us in the most tired and frail of states, can also pass on the gift of renewal. It can give us cause, in the precious time that remains, to rededicate ourselves to the commitments that matter most. Recounting those blessings and commitments is brought into magnified focus with the assistance of the journal. And since none of us will escape passing through Death's door, we can all begin these practices now. Recount your blessings. Reinvigorate your passions. Revitalize your faith. Restore your relationships.

BELOW This artist's emotionally vulnerable poetry and prose inspires the imagery for her compelling collage compositions.

Crossing Over

I crossed over
When my body no longer defined
Who I am.
More than shape, size or age.

I live life searching for meaning,
Heart and soul.

I revel in growing with knowledge that who I am is
Beyond what my body can contain.

In The Beginning

I am the one who…
Became a confused frightened girl who faced death
I am the one who…
Felt alone in the winter and stopped seeing people's faces
I am the one who…
Struggled with my spirituality
I am the one…
Who wants to leave a fingerprint in the world
I am the one who…
Is being reborn wanting life to be greener again

Something was cha
It was no
It was fluid
This gro

Other stood

Like a homele

I kept peeki

I s

I am all alo

If

The truest end of life is to know the life that never ends.

—WILLIAM PENN

ABOVE Spliced and chopped imagery illustrates the nightmares of terminal illness. Told in graphic collage and with the compilation of word and thought, the nightmare is released onto the page.

My Story

I am a woman blessed with a loving husband and six children between the ages of seven and twenty-three. In June 2003, at age forty-three, I was diagnosed with inflammatory breast cancer. After battling that, I was diagnosed in September 2005 with a GBM (glioblastoma multiforme) brain tumor, New Primary, Stage IV, terminal.

I call my artwork and poetry "Love Renewed, Spiritual Journey with Cancer." Fear and anger haunted me, and I used images and poetry to express these feelings. It allowed me to begin living with hope and to move forward. Since receiving the cancer diagnosis, my priority has been to make each day count, and this practice has been a gift to me. I am at peace with death; I enjoy the beauty around me in the relationships I have and in the new ones I will make. I laugh more heartily, to fuel my soul. I believe we have the ability to impact others by sharing our journey with them. Illness can take us through a spiritual journey that can renew our love of God and our love for family. My faith is guiding me through this journey and giving me strength to move forward. I cannot even imagine how tragic and miserable getting through life's setbacks would be, without faith. I am going to die someday, but I am not afraid.

Cancer impacts a life dramatically, but it doesn't have to end one's life, even when death is at the door. We live beyond our physical bodies. Even when cancer takes us, we continue to live. How we respond, connect, and live each day can influence others and make all the difference in how our families cope with death. We are truly more than our bodies can contain.

—Mary Zakrajsek

I Can't Escape the Rain

JOURNAL BY **Cheryl Manz**

CERTAIN THINGS IN LIFE ARE SIMPLY INESCAPABLE. We can try to make wise, healthy choices, but there will always be a factor that is out of our control. As diligently as we might try to orchestrate an existence full of wellness and joy and to steer ourselves away from hardship or pain, life will routinely insert unexpected obstacles into our daily paces. Surmounting these obstacles may bring us great, and even chronic or intense, pain. But these unplanned detours into life's lows are what define and reveal character. The painful times contrast with and define the joy and beauty that exist in our lives, as well. In these unavoidable dilemmas and disasters, we see how much others love and care for us. Although we would certainly never choose to invite the excruciating into our lives, without it, we would not grow and mature and experience the fullness of the human condition.

Pain is an opportunity to experience another facet of life, and the art journal can help you make the most of it. Use its pages to illustrate and express the view of a life seen through the magnifying glass of pain. Use its pages as a therapeutic distraction, a way to direct your mental energies toward something other than pain signals and transmission. Just as "into each life some rain must fall," so also into each life some pain must fall. In the same way rain brings growth to the green and living things around you, so can pain bring growth in you. You might one day find yourself embracing the ill weather of life, pulling out an umbrella (or your journal!) and letting it pour.

BELOW A black ground seems apropos to express the stormy and difficult period of this artist's life. Hoops of color hint at the rainbow to come.

Into each life some rain must fall.
—HENRY WADSWORTH LONGFELLOW

CREATIVE TIP

Circles add visual contrast to the straight sequences of lined paper and linear journaling. Circles cut from paper; dots created with pens, or markers, buttons, and round mini brads can add geometric variation and balance.

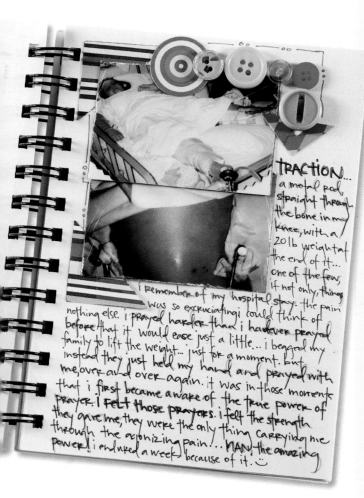

TRACTION... a metal rod, straight through the bone in my knee, with a 20lb weight at the end of it... one of the few, if not only, things I remember of my hospital stay. the pain was so excruciating i could think of nothing else. i prayed harder than i had ever prayed before that it would ease just a little... i begged my family to lift the weight... just for a moment. but instead they just held my hand and prayed with me, over and over again. it was in those moments that i first became aware of the true power of prayer. i felt those prayers. i felt the strength they gave me, they were the only thing carrying me through the agonizing pain... and the amazing power! i endured a week because of it. :)

ABOVE Colored pens help highlight particular words and phrases in this journaling entry, and the happy rainbow palette puts a hopeful frame on a difficult, painful, and unfortunate circumstance.

My Story

I was only seventeen when the accident happened. I was young, carefree, and a complete stranger to the world of medical trauma and pain that began with a life-flight helicopter landing on a hospital rooftop. But that soon changed, and during the last seven years, I became well acquainted with both. I have come to recognize the panicky feeling that settles deep inside me on the hour-and-half drive to the hospital. I have learned to despise the sterile hospital scent and the inevitably long waits while I'm there for a check-up or yet another surgery. I have listened to doctor after doctor suspect something but diagnose nothing. And I have felt the depth of emotion that comes with chronic pain and eleven unsuccessful surgeries. But what I have also felt is the amazing power of prayer—how uplifting it is to have hundreds and hundreds of people praying for you daily. I have learned endurance. I have learned to smile through heartache and to support others through their own, because of the examples provided to me throughout my ordeal. But mostly, I have learned that a little scarring (or a lot), a little pain (or a lot), and a little fear (or a lot) can actually be good for the soul. Because it teaches us that we aren't invincible. It teaches us that we can get nowhere without our faith. I'm a better woman today because of that accident. In fact, I consider it the greatest miracle in my life.

—Cheryl Manz

Why I Chose

JOURNAL BY **Allison Schubert**

THE PURSUIT OF FULL HEALTH AND WHOLENESS OF MIND AND BODY can sometimes include prescriptive interventions. Scientific and pharmaceutical advancements have provided miraculous aid to many whose bodies simply fail to produce or manage their own chemistry. Understanding and diagnosing these chemical imbalances can be confusing, and determining the appropriate healing medications can take time and tolerance. The art journal can help your physician decipher the mysterious codes of your body. Identifying specific symptoms and noting side effects in the creative journal helps you, and your doctors, enormously. Coming to terms with your body's insufficiencies can also be accomplished through the ponderings in your journal. Just as this artist uses her journal to visually get inside her head, so you, too, can employ a journal to gain access to that which resides in you.

The poets did well to conjoin music and medicine, because the office of medicine is but to tune the curious harp or man's body.

—FRANCIS BACON

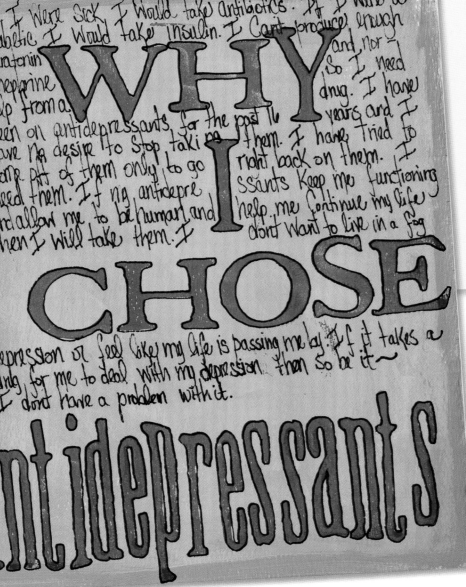
My Story

This journal entry began as a way to vent my anger and frustration about the stigma surrounding antidepressants. However, it progressed into a way of letting people know that, just because I rely on anti-depressants, it does not mean I'm weak. It means only that my brain chemicals do not function as they should. I used a scanned PET image of a depressed brain to show that depression is real and not just some sort of "pseudo-illness." I am an advo-cate of antidepressants, because they have worked so well for me. Although finding the right drug involved trial-and-error, I have found one that works wonders.

—Allison Schubert

LEFT A black-and-white photo is cut and hinged; when opened, it reveals a colorful image of the brain. The artist also used the medication packaging , whimsically cut into a crown, to top off the photo in a representation of the way in which this pharmaceutical complements her life.

Enjoy the Process

JOURNAL BY **Jamie Harper**

FINDING HEALTH AND HEALING CAN BE AN ARDUOUS PROCESS, so making it as enjoyable as possible can be pivotal to your success. The art journal is a fantastic way to find enjoyment in the process, as is demonstrated by the fanned diary seen here. The insight a journal yields can bring you great satisfaction, self-knowledge, and confidence. Converting that confidence into action can result in a functional process that brings you greater health. An artful journaling account can be colorful and creative. It need not be only lofty and figurative; it can be highly practical, as well. Regular accounts and entries contribute to cognizant living, which can lead you to concrete determinations and solid action. Watching this process unfold on the pages of your journal is entirely enjoyable, and watching the process then unfold in your life is entirely and utterly blissful.

RIGHT Pivoting open, packed with color and energy, this healing journal is an invitation to get intimate and enthused about the brass tacks of getting better.

True enjoyment comes from activity of the mind and exercise of the body; the two are ever united.

— WILHELM VON HUMBOLDT

My Story

Illness can elicit many different emotions and feelings. When I was diagnosed with fibromyalgia, from the first moment I heard the word, I was scared. I didn't know what this was or what it meant. But as I studied and researched, I was grateful to have an illness that was treatable, and to finally just know what to treat. I am grateful that I documented my many daily symptoms and struggles, so that the doctors had a clear vision of what I was suffering from and what course of action to take. Also, by keeping a journal, I was able to "talk things through" and internalize things in a meaningful and productive way. When I didn't know what I was supposed to be doing, it was as though my own words helped me learn from my mistakes and told me what to do! I guess, in a way, my journal is my friend, my cheerleader, my policeman, my solace— my life documented. This experience has truly reaffirmed to me just how important keeping a journal is. I really was healed through mine.

—Jamie Harper

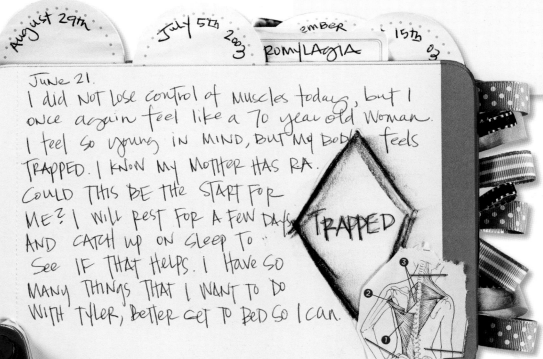

LEFT A smudgy charcoal graphic and a torn image from a magazine are simple but effective illustrations for a journal whose entries are simple but real and work through a process of reasoning to reach a healthy solution.

I Say Run

JOURNAL BY **Melissa Diekema**

DECLARATIONS AND AFFIRMATIONS ARE LIKE OFFICIAL ANNOUNCEMENTS MADE TO OURSELVES, lending clarity and conviction to the way in which we operate. When we firmly establish our motivations, we find that, though our desires may waver, rarely will they completely fail to lead us to our desired actions. When our reasons for making healthy choices are so many and so meaningful, we can be inclined to act in accord. The artist's desire to confirm her motivations for running inspired her to create the ring-bound accordion journal seen here. Using lists in your journaling can be quite helpful, and they are no less artful than traditional journaling. If you are an incessant list maker, this method of blending the analytical with the beautiful, to create a useful compendium of goals, may be the perfect creative fit for you.

BELOW An itemized list is a succinct way to sum up the reasons for your goals. A quick glance at this can be a powerful reminder to stay dedicated to health and well-being.

Do you not know that in a race all the runners run, but only one gets the prize? Run in such a way as to get the prize.

—I Corinthians 9:24 (NIV)

CREATIVE TIP

Rings and bookbinding tape can be used to create hinges and connect paneled pages together. Running ribbon through punched holes to lace pages together is another creative option. Paper can be hand-sewn or run through a sewing machine threaded with metallic or colored thread.

RIGHT Unfolded, the chipboard pages reveal the myriad choices, necessities, and pleasures that accompany the discipline of running. Photos adhered on three sides serve as pockets in which to stow more journaling.

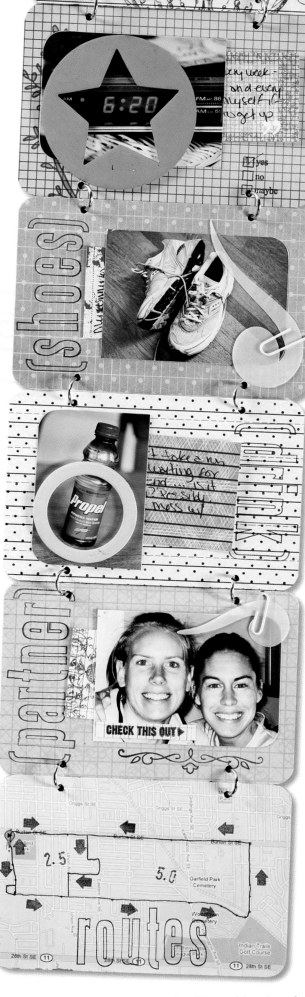

Overcoming Science

JOURNAL BY **Melissa Ackerman**

WHEN DEVESTATING ILLNESS LEAVES YOU FEELING BETRAYED by your body, an art journal can accompany you on your quest toward befriending it again. Invasive surgeries might offer you a longer lease on life, but they can also leave you in pain. You might begin to feel detached from your body and at odds with what is going on beneath your skin—and yet, making an alliance with your body is how the battle is won. A creative journal receives these conflicting feelings and helps you process what is really going on inside. Once you realize that your disease is the enemy that assaulted your body, you can partner with your body to battle the odds and "overcome the science".

Science may set limitations to knowledge but should not set limits to imagination.

—BERTRAND RUSSELL

LEFT Instead of putting title text in a typical left to right fashion, the artist took advantage of the journal's size and scale to render the text from top to bottom. By using a hodge-podge assortment of stickers to create the title, the artist makes a quick and provocative cover.

RIGHT Grounded by a single, graphic shape (the broken heart), a telling pronouncement in the word "betrayal" holds the foreground; thoughts are then scattered around this visual centerpiece.

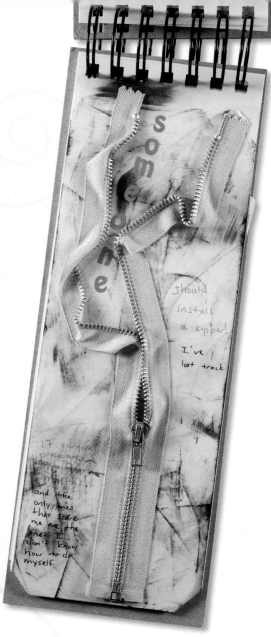

ABOVE The zipper perfectly illustrates this artist's experience of needing numerous surgeries. The long, narrow orientation of this sewing notion works beautifully with the scale of the journal.

CREATIVE TIP

Use interesting proportions to make interesting journals. Long and narrow, short and chunky: unusual paper dimensions are charming and invite intriguing treatments of art and type inside.

My Story

Before I was officially diagnosed with breast cancer, I started a journal. It had been years since I kept a journal of any sort, but I knew that this was not going to be an easy year.

I'm an obstetrician/gynecologist by profession. I did a rotation in breast surgery during my residency. So, when the technician put the screening mammogram up on the light box, I knew then and there that I had breast cancer. I knew who I needed to call, from my husband to the former mentor who would become my breast surgeon. Still, it would be another two weeks until the diagnosis was official. In the meantime, I started writing. In the earliest days, I didn't tell many people. Saying the words aloud made it too real. Keeping the words in my journal made it easier for me to deal with this disease. As treatment continued, my journal became a place to deal with the surreal world I had entered—a place in which chemotherapy drugs became more than just words in my medical books and became poisons that entered my body.

Now that I am nearing the end of active treatment, keeping an art journal has taken on a new importance. During chemotherapy and the series of surgeries (still under way), I dealt with my cancer diagnosis from the stance of a scientist. I knew the steps that needed to be taken, and I understood the science behind them intimately. I did what had to be done. There really was no other choice. I'm now reaching a point where I can deal with the emotional aspects. Smudging ink and paint on a page has become therapy. My journal is place in which I can channel the anger and sadness I pushed aside, until recently. It's also a place in which I can celebrate my life as it returns to normal, the new normal and the new me.

—Melissa Ackerman

Foreign Words and Phrases

JOURNAL BY Margert Kruljec

BELOW A canvas sample book is transformed into a journal in which artistic expression spills forth and is barely contained. Alcohol inks were used to the treat the vinyl cover, making it translucent enough to allow the journaling on the first page to be slightly visible but somewhat obscured by ethereal shades of green.

HEARING THE WORDS OF A DOCTOR'S DIAGNOSIS can be quite similar to hearing words uttered in a foreign language. They can be incomprehensible, at first. This is particularly true when our child is diagnosed with a rare illness or disability. When we venture into motherhood, it is understood that we will be responsible for our children's health and happiness, but rarely do we see ourselves caring for someone who is medically fragile. We don't even know *how* to envision them with diseases or disorders we have never even heard of. A whole culture opens up to us, one that we never knew existed before the doctors ushered us into this foreign land. Acquainting ourselves with medical terms, procedures, therapies, adaptations, and educational modifications becomes part of a new lifelong itinerary that we never signed up for. A journal can help decipher the cryptic and unfamiliar. Let your creative journal be a translator for you. It is a dependable companion and an able guide in the foreign places life takes you to.

An illness is like a journey into a far country; it sifts all one's experience and removes it to a point so remote that it appears like a vision.

—SHOLEM ASCH

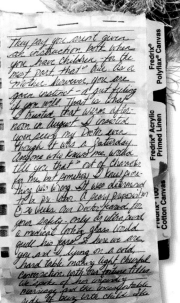

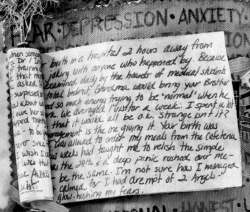

TOP Notebook pages containing extensive journaling are basted to a canvas page. With journaling pages stacked on the right, the majority of the canvas is left for a grand artistic collage.

BOTTOM An inventive pull-out scroll provides ample surface for lengthy, emotional, and detailed journaling. When pouring into words what's in your heart requires more space, inventive attachments such as this are really useful.

CREATIVE TIP

Canvas offers wonderful texture for journaling and is every bit as usable as paper. Bind letter-size canvas sheets together, to create an unusual journal. Yardage or remnants from a fabric store can also be fashioned into a journal.

My Story

A mother instinctively knows when something is wrong with her child, even if the child has yet to come into the world. Twenty-six weeks into my pregnancy, I met with my doctor and learned that my fears would be realized. There was a life-threatening problem. My daughter, Madeline, was diagnosed with hydrocephalus, resulting from the narrowing of the passageways connecting her ventricles causing a back up of fluid that was compressing her still-forming brain. To say I was in shock is an understatement. I felt like someone had punched me as hard as they could, so that I was unable to breathe. My heart broke to pieces so small, they could fit into a bag small enough to put into my pocket.

For the first two years of Madeline's life, I held my breath. As for my heart, sometimes I would pull pieces from the little bag and try to tape them back together. But my efforts were thwarted by a barrage of devastating developments. "Her head is the size of a large melon... epilepsy with grand mal seizures lasting nearly an hour... cortical visual impairment... legally blind... learning disabled... she may never walk or speak." I gave up reaching into the bag. The pain was unbearable.

But, through that pain, I became a more focused, determined mother. I learned all I could about each of her disabilities. I became her biggest advocate. Together, she and I endured countless hours of daily therapies, discovering new and innovative ways in which to help her learn to speak and to walk and to teach her brain to interpret what she saw. Along the way, I immersed myself in many organizations. I lobbied the government. I founded the country's first children's Braille library housed in a public library. I spoke to various civic groups about how they could help others in similar situations. I counseled other parents whose children had just been diagnosed with the condition.

Over time, each of these experiences in outreach gave me the courage to reach into that tiny bag. Now, however, instead of using tape, I used strands of strong leather to carefully stitch each piece together, until my heart was once again whole. Madeline is now eleven years old and has beaten all the odds. Although she will never be president or even drive a car, she can now tie her shoes, read, and do simple math. She walks, and her vocabulary is astounding. As her mother, I couldn't be more proud. On an even larger scale, this journal is a living, breathing testament that things happen for a reason. The birth of a special-needs child is a heartbreaking event, but it doesn't have to define you. It is, in fact, an offering. It is a unique opportunity to impact the lives of not only those around you, but also of those you might not otherwise have met. While it is often said that having a child such as Madeline is a blessing, I know for a fact that it is true.

—Margert Kruljec

Journaling Worksheet 3

BY MINDY CALIGUIRE

Physical Healing, Part One

"Mind over matter." What does that phrase mean? Generally, it reminds us that we are not victims of the physical tragedies that befall us or threaten to define us. Rather, there is an invisible dimension to our personhood—a dimension that continues on, even when the physical world around us (or even our own body) starts to unravel. It is this part of our person—our heart, our soul, our mind—that can be most greatly exercised in times of physical suffering. Rather that naively believing that we can mentally surmount and prevail against the physical crises in life, the gift of "mind over matter" is this: We have a life that can endure and prevail, even in the face of death. It is the interior life of the soul.

So how do you care for that inner person, particularly during times of tragedy? First, it is vitally important to acknowledge that interior self—the person you see in the mirror, but behind the eyes. This is the person who can question the suffering. Who can identify the betrayal, who can make choices about what you will think about. And, once acknowledged, to honor the needs of that soul. You can learn to hear its cries—not just the cries of the body or the cries of those around us, but the cries of the soul—your soul. What does your soul need to say? To express? To move away from?

In creating a Healing Journal of your own, you can inspire your mind as you wrestle with whatever is the matter.

- -

Reacting to the Chapter:

- Which of the journals in this chapter is most meaningful to you? Why? Look back over each one—do you identify with any of these topics? Which ones, and why?

- Which artist would you most like to have a conversation with, after seeing her journal? What would you ask her?

Reacting to Your Life:

- What physical circumstances threaten to define you right now? Be as specific as possible, writing about exactly what has happened, including memories of how you felt, what you heard, even what you dreamed or imagined.

- What colors or images do you most directly associate with these circumstances?

- What words keep coming to mind, as you move through your days?

- What do you keep telling yourself, for better or for worse?

- Write about what you are experiencing inside. Your sentences might begin with, "I may be going through _____ but what I sense inside is _____."

- Look over your response to the question above. How would you represent those interior thoughts and emotions visually? Do they have lovely arcs or jagged edges? Would they be rough, glossy, metallic, or soft?

- Be clear about the kinds of choices that still are available to you, in spite of your circumstances. What choices do you have yet to make? Which are one-time choices, and which are recurring, even daily or hourly? How might you represent these choices on paper?

The Upside

JOURNAL BY Nancy Korf

KEEPING A POSITIVE ATTITUDE IS ESSENTIAL IN SURMOUNTING CHALLENGES, yet when we are handed words like *disorder* and *disability*, their very prefixes ready us for bad news. Some disorders' names sound cruelly negative: Down syndrome, for example. (Though, to set the record straight, Down syndrome was named for Dr. John Langdon Down, who first identified it.) It would not be unreasonable to succumb to a downcast disposition when receiving such a seemingly dismal diagnosis for a forthcoming child. How do you groom a more positive response, instead? By getting information and support and looking for the upside in your situation. The creative journal can be a place to inventory the flood of information that comes in the days following a medical determination. It can also be an emotional support, a place to spill your emotions. And yes, it can help you see the sunny days ahead, even while the dark clouds loom overhead. You may have to literally craft a sun of paper and paint, but basking even in that image will bring hope to your heart and warmth to your soul. And there really is an upside to virtually everything. It may take some investigating, but in researching every angle of a diagnosis, you will find that blessed silver lining.

BELOW Layers of collaged tissue form a sun, from which journaling radiates in a grand and whimsical fashion across an entire spread of a jumbo journal.

I try to avoid looking forward or backward, and try to keep looking upward.

—CHARLOTTE BRONTË

My Story

It's hard to summarize in a paragraph or two how much this journal means to me, but since I must, I'll describe it as a written and visual document of personal metamorphosis—a transformation in my thinking, an acceptance in my heart, and the realization that what I'd first thought of as my greatest tragedy might turn out to be one of God's greatest gifts to me.

After some difficult years, which included secondary infertility, miscarriage, and a host of unsuccessful fertility treatments, we were finally pregnant with our second child. Although it felt like a new beginning, for me, it was a guarded happiness. In the back of my mind, I kept wondering what would go wrong next. I scheduled an amnio to relieve my fears and allow me to rejoice, once and for all. Unfortunately, the relief was not to come—our daughter was diagnosed with Down syndrome. The moment I heard the diagnosis, I felt the world crumble around me. This was, by far, the worst event in a string of very tough years. I started writing, expressing every thought and feeling without judgment, just letting it all come out. Then, I decided that I was ready to move forward and to learn everything I could about DS.

I contacted a mom referred to me by our geneticist; she was warm and open about her family life with their son, and her love and pride in him were obvious, even over the phone. Then, Clint and I attended a developmental seminar sponsored by the NWDSA (Northwest Down Syndrome Association), meeting dozens of local families touched by DS. What I learned was amazing and hopeful from loving families who see their children as individuals, not as diagnoses; joyous, capable children; early therapies for speech, hearing, and gross motor skills, to help educate parents and help kids reach their fullest potentials; independence, employment, and other opportunities I had never imagined were possible. Our daughter will live a good life, and we are lucky to share it with her. Now I can see again that my cup is not just half full, it runneth over.

—Nancy Korf

Aging Gracefully

JOURNAL BY Jen Nichols

AGING IS INEVITABLE, BUT IT IS NOT A SOMBER THING. The levity in this inventive journal is a vivid demonstration of that. Vitality and youthfulness are enhanced by optimism and good humor. When there is a spunk and attitude in your art journal expressions, you will find the same spunk and attitude influencing the way in which you carry yourself. Ridding yourself of the frustrations and dissatisfactions associated with advancing age allows you to leave behind the negative and embrace the positive. Nurturing your creative mind in the art journal can also open you up to creative solutions for dealing with the ticking of time. Rather than running from Senior status, you can move toward it with a full and light-hearted appreciation of the benefits and wisdom that come with age. Instead of feeling as though life is passing you by, grasp onto every waking hour with vision, energy, and laughter, through the deliberate discipline of journaling and keeping of days.

Age is a question of mind over matter.
If you don't mind, it doesn't matter.

—SATCHEL PAIGE

CREATIVE TIP

Index cards can help constitute a highly adaptable journal. Slipped into pockets, bound by rings, or kept in a box, they are easily amended and added to according to the pacing of your life and corresponding journaling.

My Story

After hitting the ripe age of forty-five, I've found that my body has started to age rapidly. I no longer see as well. My face is a long way from being smooth and clear. I can't even get my hair color to cover up the gray anymore. When my son and I go places, I find people calling me "grandma." I've even been offered the senior discount at some stores. I feel as if my life is somehow slipping away from me. I hate every gray hair and wrinkle that has appeared on my body.

What's kept me from becoming totally depressed has been my sense of humor. I'm able to poke fun at myself and have a good laugh, at the same time. My little art pages have given me a place to vent my frustrations in a humorous and slightly sarcastic fashion. These pages have been my way of making the aging process more tolerable. I can't stop myself from getting older, but at least I can try to take the sting out of it.

—Jen Nichols

ALL Versatile and easily retrievable, cleverly crafted index cards slip in and out of library pockets. High on wit and humor, they can easily be referred to when a chuckle is needed.

I Am Not a Label

JOURNAL BY **Sharon Soneff**

A DIAGNOSIS CAN BE IMMENSELY EMPOWERING. It can be an answer to nagging questions. It can be a key to unlocking doors that were jammed shut. It can set you on a path of remedy and recovery. A diagnosis can identify what was once a baffling mystery. It can be a step toward positive action, not a sentence. But, when diagnostic information is used to inappropriately label people, especially by one's self, what should be helpful can be damning and damaging. Learning to see a diagnosis in its proper context is important.

This journal was created by a mother with and for her teen son, to help him make sense of how he and others should view himself in the context of his diagnosis. A diagnosis is not meant to define a person but, rather, lend understanding. It is not meant to prejudge or predetermine one's future— it's meant to optimize it. Whether you need to sort out a difficult diagnosis of your own or to help a child or friend through his or her own diagnostic wilderness, the art journal can be an source of comfort and understanding.

LEFT A name badge and bold, broad-tipped markers were used to graphically demonstrate the intent of this journal. Pastels and paint are also employed for a portrait, underlining the message that there is a face and a person to which the diagnosis has been applied. Humanizing and personalizing diagnostic information helps to move it away from being a confining label.

Happy is he who has been able to learn the causes of things.

—VIRGIL

My Story

It has been nearly ten years since my son was assessed and diagnosed with Asperger's syndrome. At the time, he was four years old, and the news came as both a shock and a relief. For, in identifying Ian's disorder, we found a way to treat his symptoms. We immediately became pro-active and plunged into a myriad of early interventions. I'm so thankful that we did not wallow in a period of denial, because our quick, aggressive action, combined with Ian's hard work, truly paid off. Today, at fourteen, Ian has shed many of the traits of his syndrome and is functioning beautifully at his local public school. However, the diagnosis that was once a godsend is now something that my son finds stifling and disdainful. I struggle between respecting his point of view and wanting to help him come to terms with his neurological disorder. Keeping this journal with and for him has been a way for me to do both: it is a visual demonstration that Asperger's is not who he is but merely one small piece of information about him.

—Sharon Soneff

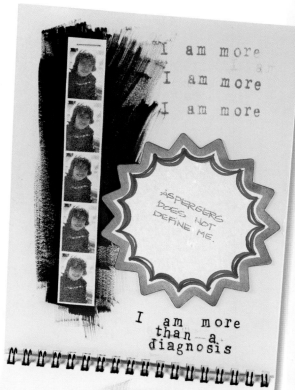

LEFT Repetition, an effective design technique, is employed through both phrases and photos. Not only does this create a strong design, it also reiterates the powerful message of the journaling.

A Journey of Hope

JOURNAL BY **Kate Teague**

THE WORDS "HOPE" AND "ILLNESS" ARE RARELY UTTERED IN THE SAME BREATH. They can routinely coexist, however, in a book devoted to creative healing. Let an art journal be home to words that elicit courage from you. Arranging inspirational quotations in an artful array, as in the unique spread of journal pages here, can bring you full circle. Whether at the origin or at the end of your journey, there will always be the constants: you, your journal, and your faith, acting as buoyant navigators throughout your expedition. In devoting time, thought, and energy toward the written words of hope, you are nurturing the development of possibility and promise in the midst of illness. The words committed to page will also linger in the mind, making hope and illness unlikely friends inside your own frame.

While there's life, there's hope.

—ANONYMOUS

RIGHT Each page of this fanned deck-style journal holds emotion and an inspirational quote. Individually, each page contributes a unique thought; together, they result in an enchanting visual.

CREATIVE TIP

Clear epoxy stickers
can be adhered over
journaling to draw
attention to significant
words. A do-it-yourself
substitution is to apply
clear-drying, dimensional
glue over key words
and phrases.

My Story

When I first found out I had multiple sclerosis, it was a huge blow. It knocked me down. I was tired, and I was sick. During the recovery phase from my first major episode, I turned to scrapbooking and art as a way of healing. I threw myself into it. Being off work gave me a lot of time on my hands, and I didn't want to spend that time feeling sorry for myself. It's not in my nature. So, I found myself immersed in what I call my art. When I made this little book, I wanted it to be a source of inspiration—little collection of quotes to uplift me and give me strength whenever I needed a little boost.

The process of finding quotes was in itself healing. I read inspirational quotes on websites and found a few great books at the library. This portion of making my book reminded me of the power of positive thinking and reinforced my desire to not let my diagnosis control my life in a negative way. When I created the book, I wanted to keep it small, so it could sit it on my nightstand table as a nightly reminder of where I have been and how far I have come. I am proud of the fact that, yes, I have been diagnosed with a life-altering disease, but I haven't let it control me. I have found a way to deal with the emotions that come along with it, and knowing that has given me so much strength.

—Kate Teague

So Small and Fragile

JOURNAL BY Tammy Kay

Life is brimming with amazingly paradoxical revelations about how we are simultaneously incredibly strong and resilient and markedly small and fragile. Never has this been more true than with newborn babes, especially those born prematurely. Neonatal wards hold precious living examples of our capability to survive and thrive against medical odds. Bearing witness to this, and experiencing it firsthand, is a life-altering occurrence. Being the mother of a babe that hangs in that tension can be terrifying and traumatic. The newborn we envisioned bringing home to a nursery is instead left behind at the hospital in intensive care. The child we nurtured and bonded with in the womb, whom we longed to hold in our arms, might instead lie in the embrace of an incubator.

The emptiness of your arms and the sadness of your heart can be described in the journal, where you are free to unleash and release your fears and sadness. The numerous hours spent in a hospital are entirely conducive to art journaling. When life seems more fragile than strong, and when we are diminished by the enormity of our situation, the journal brings it all into perspective. When a child's difficult start spurs a mother toward overprotection and unfounded worry, the journal can, once again, help her to move on, letting her and her offspring make the steps and falls that earmark healthy, normal development.

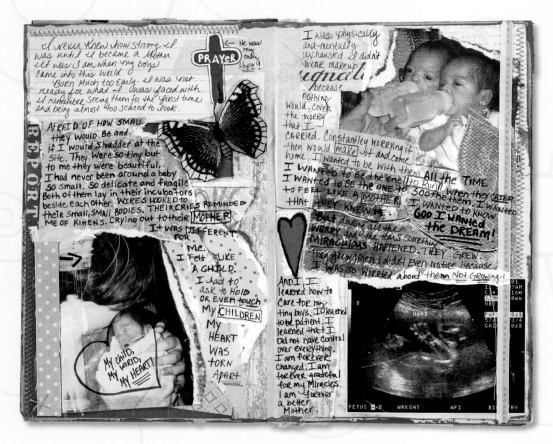

LEFT Paper tearing is a technique employed in this journal, in which photos, illustrations, and even an embroidered patch overlap one another.

*It is sometimes the most fragile
things that have the power to endure
and become sources of strength.*

—MAY SARTON

BELOW Ribbons and
tapes printed with
measuring-tape motifs
emphasize the journal's
theme of the tiny size
of premature babies.

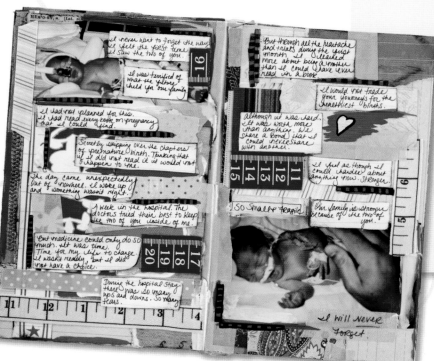

My Story

For years, I have had pictures tucked
away, just waiting for my story to be
told. After five years, it is still hard for
me to look at pictures of when my boys
were first born. So many emotions and
memories flood my mind. I knew, though,
that if I was avoiding these photos and
this chapter of my life, it was something
I needed to address. When I started the
process of telling my story, the memories
and emotions came, but, in them, I found
a different woman, one who is older and
much more mature. A woman who would
not trade her story for anything. A
woman who is touched by other people's
stories of premature birth. When I hear
of someone facing the same issues that
my boys did, my heart aches for them.
When I sat down and worked on my
journal, I tried to remember those women.
I try to remember that life is a journey,
and there will always be
someone who travels down the
same road as me. Reflecting on
my boys' birth has put closure
to a story that was waiting to
be told. I feel like a chapter of
my life has finally ended.

—Tammy Kay

A Spectrum of Choices

JOURNAL BY **Sharon Soneff**

A HEALTHY LIFESTYLE IS ACHIEVED, NOT OVERNIGHT, NOR IN A SINGLE MOMENT, but through a series of good choices. Each good choice, built upon another, compounds and assimilates into a healthy life. Of course, there will always be setbacks, and times when we opt for the inferior choice, but each new choice offers an opportunity to correct our missteps. When the innumerable choices we face are contemplated all at once, it can be overwhelming. But broken down into single, isolated choices, creating a healthy lifestyle becomes entirely achievable. Here, a colorful journal uses hue to encourage healthy thinking and to consider making better choices. The multihued platform of this book alludes to the fact that our choices are really as infinite and varied as the colors of the

spectrum. Using the creative diary to illustrate and fashion our choices helps us cement them into our behavioral thinking and choose what's best for us in the practical, functioning realm of our daily living. When we learn to operate with healthful decisiveness, that spectrum of choice is a beautiful and wondrous prism in our lives.

LEFT Black gesso is brushed onto the album's surface, except for a central area that exposes the original striped fabric. There, opaque markers were used to pen the journal's title. Inside, pages divided into blocks of vivid color provide unique organization for correlating entries.

Life is a sum of all your choices.

—ALBERT CAMUS

okra
peas
spinach
zuchini

think
Green

5 a day

Momma always said
EAT YOUR PEAS

&
artichokes
arugala
asparagus
broccoli
brussels sprouts
cabbage
celery
cucumbers
endive
leeks
lettuce

ABOVE A monochromatic layering of color makes an effective visual that echoes the content of the journaling. Using multiple mediums (pen, colored pencil, and acrylic) also adds visual interest.

CREATIVE TIP

Gesso is a staple in an artist's pantry. This opaque medium, available in white and black, primes and covers almost any surface, readying it for recycling, renewal, and alteration. Use it to transform slick surfaces to matte or to cover the color or text of an existing surface to receive a new color and fresh text.

health and healing for the body   **121**

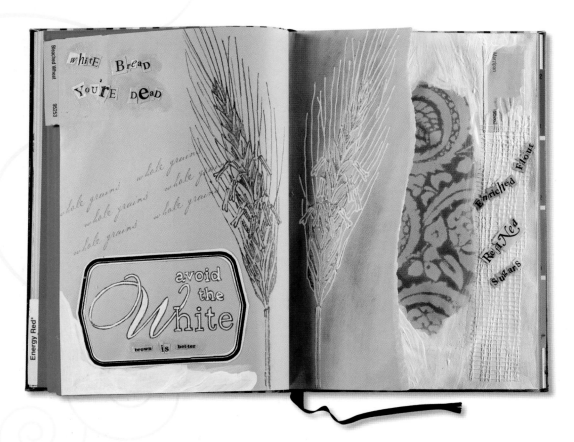

TOP Tearing a page creates a dynamic entry, in which the top page works in tandem with the page beneath. White gesso, netted handmade paper, and letters clipped from vintage books add intrigue.

BOTTOM A paint chip with varied shades of orange creates a sidebar panel of tone-on-tone, in which illustrations, ephemera, and patterning create a composition that is playful and random in counterpoint.

Journaling Worksheet 4

BY MINDY CALIGUIRE

Physical Healing, Part Two

Whether we categorize ourselves as weak-willed or strong-willed, each of us has a central part of the human person lodged deep inside the soul: a will. The part of us that chooses. The part that says, "I will" or "I will not!"

Choosing is an essential part of daily living, and, undoubtedly, we make hundreds of choices each and every day. One of the most difficult places for a human soul to thrive, though is in an environment in which our choices seem limited. And in times of suffering and tragedy, our choices do become limited. We did not choose to have a child run away. We did not choose a particular diagnosis. We did not choose to be adandoned or betrayed; we did not choose our genes or family of origin. Truly, some of the most defining events of our lives are beyond our choosing. Our will simply does not factor into the equation at all.

When our choices are limited, we can begin to feel trapped, hopeless, and sometimes even doomed. A remarkable attribute of those who endured slavery or wrongful imprisonment or debilitating disease, though, is the human capacity to make wise and life-giving choices, even under the most heinous of circumstances. The Harriet Tubmans, the Nelson Mandelas, the Christopher Reeves. These folks become our heroes! And so they should. They overcame their physical limitations and became agents of freedom, hope, life, and inspiration.

Each of us can become everyday heroes when we exercise our choices for good—no matter the circumstances before us. When you create a healing journal that acknowledges the choices you are making—and asks for the help you need in making future choices—you are on the journey of becoming just such a hero.

Reacting to the Chapter:

• Which project spoke to you directly? Why?

• What choices did you see being made by the artists as they faced their particular challenges?

• In what way do you imagine the choices they made helped them?

• How might they have been tempted to collapse under the weight of their circumstances?

Reacting to Your Life:

• In what area of your life have you felt trapped, hopeless, or doomed?

• Write about some of the choices you daily have in front of you.

• What choices do you feel have been taken from you? How do you find yourself responding to those losses?

• Who or what inspires you to keep going in a position direction each day?

• What issues are you passionate about and willing to fight for—how do they relate to your circumstances?

• What role does courage play in your life, as you face these choices? What role does faith play? What role does community (meaningful connections to others) play?

• How would you represent your options visually?

Resources

3M
www.3M.com
Adhesives, laminating supplies, and transparencies

7 Gypsies
www.7gypsies.com
Albums, journals, paper, and embellishments

AC Moore
www.acmoore.com
Art and craft supplies

Aaron Brothers Art & Framing
www.aaronbrothers.com
Albums, journals, and art supplies

American Crafts
www.americancrafts.com
Albums, papers, stickers, embellishments, pens, and markers

Arizona Art Supply
www.arizonaartsupply.com
Art supplies

ArtCity
www.artcity.com
Art and craft supplies, frames, and furniture

All My Memories
www.allmymemories.com
Paper, ribbon, and other scrapbook supplies

Altered Pages
www.alteredpages.com
Ephemera products, scrapbook, and collage supplies

American Crafts
www.americancrafts.com
Paper, vellum, embellishments, pens, markers, and cards

ArtChix
www.artchixstudio.com
Vintage images, rubber stamps, transparencies, paper, and embellishments

Autumn Leaves
www.autumnleaves.com
Paper, transparencies, embellishments, and books

Avery
www.avery.com
Tags, labels, and office supplies

Barnes and Noble
www.barnesandnoble.com
Bookseller: merchandise includes blank journals

Basic Grey
www.basicgrey.com
Paper, stickers, chipboard, and embellishments

Bazzill
www.bazzillbasics.com
Cardstock

Borders
www.borders.com
Bookseller: merchandise includes blank journals

C. R. Gibson
www.crgibson.com
Albums, journals, and decorative papers

Carolee's Creations
www.carolees.com
Decorative paper and embellishments

Chatterbox
www.chatterboxinc.com
Paper and embellishments

Creative Imaginations
www.cigift.com
Decorative paper, supplies, and embellishments

Daisy Ds
www.daisydspaper.com
Decorative paper

Delta
www.deltacrafts.com
Acrylic paint and craft supplies

Dick Blick Art materials
www.dickblick.com
Art supplies

EK Success
www.eksuccess.com
Patterned paper, supplies, and embellishments

Fancy Pants
www.fancypantsdesigns.com
Chipboard

Fiskars
www.fiskars.com
Scissors, deckle-edge scissors, and other cutting tools

Fontwerks
www.fontwerks.com
Paper, ribbon, and rubber stamps

Found Elements
foundelements.com
Vintage items, ephemera, collage supplies

Glue Dots International
www.gluedotsinternational.com
Adhesive dots for paper craft applications

Golden Artist Colors
www.goldenpaints.com
Paints, gel mediums, gesso, gels, grounds, and varnishes

Heidi Swapp
www.heidiswapp.com
Paper-crafting products

Hero Arts
www.heroarts.com
Stamps and embellishments

Hobby Lobby
www.hobbylobby.com
Craft supplies

Jacquard
www.jacquardproducts.com
Paints and pearlescent powders

Jo-Ann Fabric & Crafts
www.joann.com
Fabric, scrapbook, and craft supplies

Judikins
www.judikins.com
Rubber stamps, supplies, and Diamond Glaze

Junkitz
www.junkitz.com
Papers, transparencies, stickers, and embellishments

KI Memories
www.kimemories.com
Albums, scrapbook paper, supplies, and embellishments

K & Company
www.kandcompany.com
Albums, paper, stickers, and embellishments

Karen Foster Design
www.karenfosterdesign.com
Scrapbook paper, stickers, and embellishments

Kolo
www.kolo.com
Albums, presentation binders, scrapbooks, and storage boxes

Krylon
www.krylon.com
Spray and brush-on paints and finishes

Lazar Studiowerx
www.lazarstudiowerx.com
Decorative papers, die cuts, rub-ons, fiber, and stamps

Li'l Davis
www.lildavisdesigns.com
Paper, stickers, and embellishments

Liquitex
www.liquitex.com
Paint and craft finishes

Making Memories
www.makingmemories.com
Scrapbook paper, tools, supplies, and embellishments

Manto Fev
www.mantofev.com
Collage and assemblage art supplies

Marvy Uchida
www.uchida.com
Markers, ink, and hole punches

May Arts
www.mayarts.com
Ribbon

Maya Road
www.mayaroad.com
Ribbon, fiber, stickers, chipboard, and embellishments

Me and My Big Ideas
www.meandmybigideas.com
Albums, papers, stickers, rub-ons, and embellishments

Michael's
www.michaels.com
Art and craft supplies

Moleskines
www.moleskines.com
Journals

My Mind's Eye
www.mymindseyeinc.com
Scrapbook paper, die-cut alphabets and frames, rub-ons, and stickers

Office Depot
www.officedepot.com
Office supplies

Offray
www.offray.com
Ribbon

Paperblanks
www.paperblanks.com
Exquisite blank journals and books

Paper Source
www.paper-source.com
Paper and stationery, rubber stamps, book binding supplies, journals, and albums

Papier Valise
www.papiervalise.com
Mixed media supplies

Pearl Paint
www.pearlpaint.com
Art supplies

Paper Addict
www.paperaddict.com
Scrapbook paper

Paper Style
www.paperstyle.com
Scrapbook supplies, invitations, and stationery

Plaid
www.plaidenterprises.com
Acrylic paint, stamps, paper, and tools

Prism
www.prismpapers.com
Fine cardstock

Provo Craft
www.provocraft.com
Cutting systems and tools, paper, stickers, embellishments, and albums

Ranger
www.rangerink.com
Ink, ink pads, and related products

Rex Art
www.rexart.com
Art supplies

Rubber Stampede
www.rubberstampede.com
Rubber stamps and art stamps

Rusty Pickle
www.rustypickle.com
Albums, hardware, ink, leather, lace, paper, ribbon, stamps, stickers, and tags

Sakura
www.sakura.com
Archival pens and markers

Sanford
www.sanford.com
Sharpie markers

Scenic Route
www.scenicroutepaper.com
Paper, stickers, rub-on transfers, chipboard, and embellishments

Scrap Artist
www.scrapartist.com
Digital kits, digital papers, digital embellishments, and community

ScrapWorks
www.scrapworks.com
Scrapbook paper, tools, supplies, and embellishments

Stampington & Company
www.stampington.com
Rubber stamp and collage art supplies

Staples
www.staples.com
Scrapbook papers and albums, office supplies

Stickers Galore
www.stickersgalore.com
Stickers

Target
www.target.com
Home accessories and stationery supplies

Therm O Web
www.thermoweb.com
Adhesives

Toothfaeries
www.popplagid.com
Moleskin notebooks with hand-printed artwork by Toothfaeries and Sigur Rós

Two Peas in a Bucket
www.twopeasinabucket.com
Scrapbook supplies, fonts, digital kits, ideas, and community

X-Acto
www.hunt-corp.com
Knives and blades

Xyron, Inc.
www.xyron.com
Adhesive application machines, cutting and printing tools

Walnut Hollow
www.walnuthollow.com
Wood embellishments

Westrim
www.westrimcrafts.com
Scrapbook and paper-art embellishments

Working Class Studio
www.shopscadonline.com
Artist-driven and -developed products by the Savannah College of Art and Design. Merchandise includes journals, stationery, and more

Contributors

Melissa Ackerman
Melissa is a New Jersey–based, board-certified ob/gyn. Married to her college sweetheart, this mom of one has been an avid journaler, scrapbooker, and crafter for most of the last decade. Her designs have appeared in various books and magazines, including Creating Keepsakes, Simple Scrapbooks, and Memory Makers magazine. Her blog, at www.melissaga.blogspot.com, chronicles her journey as a young breast cancer survivor.

Carol Banks
Carol incorporates techniques from her many creative interests into her journals, scrapbooks, and altered art projects. Since 1999, Carol's work has been published in a variety of magazines, including Creating Keepsakes, Scrapbooks, Etc., and the Simple Scrapbooks Kits and Coordinates book. She has received an Honorable Mention in the Creating Keepsakes Hall of Fame three years in a row (2000 to 2002). Carol lives an adventurous life with her army chaplain husband, Kevin, and their three children.
www.embracetheadventure.blogspot.com
www.cardsforsoldiers.blogspot.com
carol.l.banks@gmail.com

Rebecca Brown
Rebecca only recently began exploring the art journal medium, integrating her other long term passions: writing stories, plays, and poetry. Rebecca bid farewell to her part-time job as a drama teacher, when she, her husband, and three children left their hometown of Perth, Western Australia, and started a new adventure in the United States.
http://brownart.typepad.com

Danea Burleson
Danea discovered scrapbooking and art journals in 1997, and in 2004, after winning a layout contest for a Creating Keepsakes University Cruise, was introduced to the professional side of the crafting industry. She designed and taught for Creative Imaginations and now designs for Technique Tuesday, a clear stamp company. Despite multiple hand surgeries from rheumatoid arthritis deterioration, Danea rarely slows down. Danea lives in Northern California with her husband, Jeff, and their first child, a baby boy.
www.scrappetite.com

Mindy Caliguire
Mindy and her husband, Jeff, planted a church in the Boston area, where she served in a variety of leadership roles for ten years and launched Soul Care (www.soulcare.com), dedicated to helping people restore health to their souls. She served in the area of spiritual formation at Willow Creek Community Church from 2001 to 2004. In 2005, she re-engaged with Soul Care, serving churches and organizations through leadership consulting and retreats. Mindy is Midwest regional director for the Spiritual Formation Alliance, building partnerships and creating formational events. Whether formally or informally, Mindy mentors leaders, focusing on re-establishing their spiritual vitality as the primary step towards a lifestyle of sustainable ministry and leadership.

Rachel Denbow
Rachel loves soy milk, Chapstick, red mary janes, vintage textiles, indie music, sunshine, trips to small towns, and making it herself. She lives in California with her handsome husband and beautiful son. She is a part of Red Velvet Art and head designer for the Red Velvet Kit Club. She has been published in Scrap City, by Paul Gambino, as well as in Faith Books and Spiritual Journaling, by Sharon Soneff.
www.blingonmysewingmachine.blogspot.com.

Genine Devlahovich
Genine has been a lover of arts and crafts since she was young and her mother held a weekly "Arts and Crafts" event. She owned a scrapbook store for five years, but, after her bout with breast cancer, she decided to close it and spend more time with her family. Now, she dabbles in photography and is an education director, promoting, organizing, and teaching classes at a local scrapbook store. She also is an advocate for Young Survivors of Breast Cancer. She also donates a portion of the business profits from her travel agency to help find a cure (www.traveling4acure.com). Genine makes an effort to help anyone in her path who is facing breast cancer.
housemouse007@roadrunner.com

Melissa Diekema
Melissa is a professional photographer with a passion for candid photography of people of all ages. She enjoys scrapbooking and stamping, in addition to journaling. She is on the Fontwerks design team and a freelance writer for Better Homes and Gardens and Scrapbooks, Etc. Her work can be seen in Quarry Books' Faithbooks and Spiritual Journaling. She lives with her husband, Paul, and their three children in Michigan.
www.melissadiekemaphotography.com

Liz Eaton
Liz has always been in love with creating and making art, from metal arts and jewelry making to, more recently, paper arts and scrapbooking. Through her friend and industry innovator, Heidi Swapp, she was introduced to the medium, working as a product designer for Heidi's company for two years. Liz now has her own website, theanywherestudio.com, which provides online kits and classes, in which people can create, connect, and grow.
lizeaton.typepad.com.

Emily Falconbridge
Emily is a free spirit, with a love for color, texture, playing with paints, and being outside. She is a woman in love with her family, and fuels her creative passion by creating handmade scrapbooks and journal pages. Emily teaches workshops nationally and internationally, is a regular contributor to the Autumn Leaves Designing With book series, and is a Garden Girl design team member.
www.twopeasinabucket.com.
www.embers.typepad.com.

Jamie Harper
Jamie Harper has been mixing art into journals, scrapbooks, and projects for the past twelve years. She loves to try any new and exciting craft, and as a photographer aims to capture the true spirit of a subject. Jamie, her husband, and four children live in Arizona. Her work has appeared in many publications, including Creating Keepsakes, Scrapbooks Etc., Memory Makers, and Scrapbook Trends. She has also co-authored two e-books from scrapbook.com and is a recent inductee to the 2007 Creating Keepsakes Hall of Fame.
www.harperaz6@yahoo.com

Marilyn Healey
With a degree in illustration, Marilyn has worked as an artist in one form or another for many years. Ten years ago, scrapbooking and art journaling began to take over her life. She was inducted into the Creating Keepsakes Hall of Fame in 2000 and the PaperKuts Power Team in 2001. Marilyn has been on several design teams for scrapbooking companies, such as Autumn Leaves, KI Memories, and Provo Craft and was a Garden Girl on Two Peas In A Bucket website for four years. Marilyn has been published in numerous industry magazines, most recently with Autumn Leaves' Designing With and Foof-A-Life publications. She lives in Eagle Mountain, Utah, with her husband and their four kids.
http://marilynhealey.blogspot.com/

Tammy Kay
Tammy is a dreamer. She always has ten ideas in her mind at one time. As a child, her favorite pastimes were coloring and pretending. Today, she is a wife and mother of three amazing children. After spending most of her day tending to her twin boys and little girl, she finds peace and quiet sitting down with art supplies at hand. Tammy is a designer for Creative Imaginations.
www.tammykay.typepad.com

Nancy Korf
Nancy's interest in journaling began with a middle school assignment to write the story of her life. Over the next few years, her interests in journaling, scrapbooking, and rubber stamping blossomed. A runner up in the 2004 Memory

Makers Masters contest, she is currently on the design team for Boxer Scrapbooks and Pazzles, and her work has appeared in both scrapbooking and rubberstamping publications. With masters' degrees in business and income taxation, Nancy left her eleven-year career in international tax to stay at home with her son, Connor, and new baby, Makena, the star of Nancy's healing journal.
www.scrapbookresumes.com
nancykorf@gmail.com

Margert Kruljec
A freelance designer, Margert creates, writes, and teaches mixed-media and altered art for Altered Arts magazine and several industry manufacturers. Her specialties include paper crafts, memory crafts, wearable art, mixed-media collage, and altered/outsider art. She travels to teach all over the country. Margert's work has appeared in Altered Arts, Somerset Studio, Legacy, Memory Makers, PaperWorks, and Paper Crafts magazines, as well as publications by Soho Publishing, DRG Publishing, Kalmbach Publishing, Lark Publishing, Pinecone Press, and Ivy Cottage. Margert and her family live in the beautiful mountains of West Virginia.
www.mementosdiarte.com

Tammy Kushnir
Tammy has been an artist all of her life. She began drawing portraits and ended up falling in love with mixed-media/altered books. She is now finding ways to ways to balance her two loves—her family and art—while staying home with her small children. Her work can be seen in several Stampington & Company publications, such as Somerset Studio, Somerset Memories (formerly Legacy), as well as in Stampington's special publications Transparent Art, Somerset Home, Somerset Weddings III, Somerset Gallery (Summer Edition 2007), and the upcoming Somerset Holidays. She lives in Philadelphia with her two small boys and an understanding husband.
www.itsmysite.com/tammykushnir

Shimelle Laine
Shimelle grew up in Middle America, went to England to study literature, and never made it back home. Always passionate about writing and crafting, Shimelle was inducted into the Creating Keepsakes Hall of Fame in 2001 before joining the team of Britain's best-selling scrapbook magazine, ScrapBook Inspirations, where she works today. Her series of mixed-media art, Guide Words, went on to become a book and, in 2004, her first online class. Since then, her website, www.shimelle.com, has allowed her to work with thousands of creative women, through it's unique classes on art journaling, documenting holidays and traditions, and writing the story of the life you want to lead. She is currently planning her upcoming London wedding.
shimelle@writtendown.com

Cheryl Manz
Cheryl works in Chicago as a nanny and freelance scrapbooker. She tries to express her love of life through her pages by using bright, colorful designs and meaningful journaling in each and every creation. She began scrapbooking seven years ago, after a life-changing automobile accident that resulted in eleven surgeries over the years that left her in almost constant pain. Scrapbooking and journaling have become her therapy, an outlet for the frustration of chronic pain. Cheryl is on the design teams for Scenic Route Paper Company and American Crafts and also does freelance work.
www.cherylmanz.typepad.com.

Jen Nichols
Jen, a seventh grade science teacher, is a crafter at heart. Even as a little girl, Jen was always busy creating works of art and dreamed of attending art school. Art school didn't happen, but the enthusiasm she had for crafting never faded. Jen, who has been a member of several scrapbook design teams, is a member of the design team at www.creativexpress.com. Jen has been published in various books and magazines, including Memory Makers, Creating Keepsakes, Paper Trends, Paperkuts, and Cards. She lives in northern Indiana with her husband and son.
nicholjen@gmail.com

Deb Perry
Being a wife and mom to three busy teens keeps her on her toes, but Deb feels as long as she has breath, she'll be creating something every day, whether by drawing, painting, scrapbooking, altered art, or photography. Recently, computer design was added to that mix. Deb is a Fiskars Top Ten design team member and freelances for several other companies. Creating Keepsakes and Memory Makers magazines have published her work regularly, and she has been a contributing artist to eight books. She also contributed to Sharon's 2006 book, Faith Books and Spiritual Journaling.
debperry@gmail.com

Allison Schubert
Allison resides in Easley, South Carolina, with her husband, her four-year-old daughter, and a long-haired dachshund. She comes from a long line of strong artists, finding photography as her own art form in high school. Later, after the birth of her daughter, she discovered art journals and scrapbooking, which combine her love of photography with paper arts. Allison is on a personal mission to take scrapbooking to a higher level of purpose and artistry. Allison also does design work for Creative Imaginations.
mdschubert@charter.net

Karan Simoni
Karan has been a freelance scrapbook designer since 1998. Her work has been featured in Creating Keepsakes and Scrapbooks Etc. magazines. Her current passion is mixed-media art combined with spiritual journaling workshops. She teaches at The Place, in Pleasant Hill, California, a spiritual healing center. She holds weekend workshops on Art Journals and Spirit Dolls in the heart of the Livermore wine country. Karan lives in Martinez, California, with her husband and four children.
karansimoni@comcast.net

Janelle Simons
With creative endeavors ranging from jewelry making to floral designs, Janelle's hands are always busy. These days, her creativity is put to task as a wife, and mother to the beautiful five children she home-schools. Janelle has devoted her scant spare time to sharing her experiences of walking through physical and emotional challenges with other women, praying and mentoring with those who now face dilemmas similar to her own. Residing in Southern California, she enjoys gardening, baking, and sharing tea with friends.

Kate Teague
Kate Teague is a multi-media artist at heart. She loves that journals and scrapbooks give her the creative liberty to mix everything from photos and paper to digital elements. Kate is on the creative team for Digital Scrapbooking Magazine and the Shutterfly digital advisory team and is a Garden Girl for www.twopeasinabucket.com. She also is a product designer for Fontwerks, Inc. She lives in Canada with her husband of ten years and her four-year-old daughter.
http://kate_teague.typepad.com

Mary Zakrajsek
Mary was a paper lover and a collage artist at heart. If you gave her some paper, scissors, and glue, you'd be amazed at the outcome! She loved to create art with magazine images, cards she received, and found objects. Mary also wrote profound poetry to accompany her artwork as a way to further express her feelings. Mary survived breast cancer survivor only to be diagnosed with a GBM terminal brain tumor. But through difficult days, she still maintained an infectious laugh and a witty sense of humor. But it was her faith and family that were the two loves of her life. In Carmel, Indiana, Mary is survived by her wonderful husband, Mick, whose unconditional love gave her great sustenance, both physically and emotionally. Also carrying on with the love and faith their mother instilled in them are Mary's six children: Catherine, Jessica, Michael, Robert, David, and Mary Grace.

About the Author

SHARON SONEFF is a wife and mother of two, residing in a coastal town of Southern California. With a simple devotion for the arts and a passion to honor God with her humble gifts, Sharon encourages others around the globe to use the arts to elevate and enhance their own lives. Partial to watercolors and the lettering arts, Sharon also explores various mixed media. When she brings her brush to paper, she also brings to it her love for nature, architecture, and literature. Her background in interior design and as a colorist also factor into her design savvy.

Being featured in numerous publications and then inducted into the Creating Keepsakes Hall of Fame, serendipitously set Sharon off on a path she had not previously planned or expected to take. Sharon's introduction of scrapbook papers and stickers into the crafting marketplace, with the debut of her flagship brand, Sonnets™, has blossomed into Sonnets Studios™, which encompasses a substantial body of artwork, several distinct brands, and a vast array of products. Her brand includes gift wrap, greeting cards, mugs, photo frames, and seasonal gifts and holiday decor. Sharon enjoys being absorbed in every detail of product design, from the conception of the silhouette to the surface art. Sharon, a gifted writer and speaker, always finds a way to construe beauty and inspiration from the commonplace and ordinary. Look for her previous title, *Faith Books and Spiritual Journaling: Expressions of Faith through Art*, also from Quarry books. Find out more about Sharon Soneff at her site, **www.sonnetsstudios.com**.

Acknowledgments

I WANT TO THANK MY CONTRIBUTORS, for not only agreeing to part with their priceless and personal artwork but for also sharing their struggles, in the hope of helping others with theirs. Their willingness to share my vision buoyed me, and the beauty of their art inspired me. Each of them is a unique gem to me and to this project. I am profoundly grateful for my editor, Mary Ann Hall. I'm sure I tested her patience to new levels with this project, when I struggled with the magnitude of the material. It was so important to me to do it justice, and this responsibility weighed heavily on me. But Mary Ann's forbearance and encouragement helped to press on when I wasn't certain that I could.

I must thank Mindy Caliguire, because my appreciation for her runs deep. Without her, this book may have been pretty and inspirational but not nearly as practical. The additions of her thoughtful worksheets help us all make the connections from the preceding pages to the distinct challenges in our own lives. Because of Mindy, we do not merely recognize from a distance the difficulties of the artists in the book, we are better able to relate to the matter of the book, addressing and owning our own physical and emotional difficulties.

Finally, I would like to thank my husband, Gerry. Thank you for putting your blessing on this project, allowing me to share publicly our personal hardships. This book is a testament to how strong we are and how much we have weathered. The storms we have endured have battered us at times but have never defeated us. I couldn't love you more or be more grateful for what God has forged in us individually and as a couple.